MILESTONES
IN AMERICAN HISTORY

THE EMANCIPATION
PROCLAMATION

MILESTONES
IN
AMERICAN HISTORY

THE ACQUISITION OF FLORIDA

THE ALAMO

ALEXANDER GRAHAM BELL
AND THE TELEPHONE

THE ATTACK ON PEARL HARBOR

THE CALIFORNIA GOLD RUSH

THE CIVIL RIGHTS ACT OF 1964

THE DONNER PARTY

THE ELECTRIC LIGHT

THE EMANCIPATION PROCLAMATION

THE ERIE CANAL

THE LOUISIANA PURCHASE

MANIFEST DESTINY

THE MONROE DOCTRINE

THE OREGON TRAIL

THE OUTBREAK OF THE CIVIL WAR

THE PONY EXPRESS

THE PROHIBITION ERA

THE ROBBER BARONS AND THE
SHERMAN ANTITRUST ACT

THE SINKING OF THE USS *MAINE*

SPUTNIK/EXPLORER I

THE STOCK MARKET CRASH OF 1929

THE TRANSCONTINENTAL RAILROAD

THE TREATY OF PARIS

THE WRIGHT BROTHERS

THE EMANCIPATION PROCLAMATION

ENDING SLAVERY IN AMERICA

ADAM WOOG

CHELSEA HOUSE PUBLISHERS

An imprint of Infobase Publishing

The Emancipation Proclamation

Copyright © 2009 by Infobase Publishing

All rights reserved. No part of this book may be reproduced or utilized in any form or by any means, electronic or mechanical, including photocopying, recording, or by any information storage or retrieval systems, without permission in writing from the publisher. For information, contact:

Chelsea House
An imprint of Infobase Publishing
132 West 31st Street
New York, NY 10001

Library of Congress Cataloging-in-Publication Data

Woog, Adam, 1953–
  The Emancipation Proclamation : ending slavery in America / Adam Woog.
    p. cm. — (Milestones in American history)
  Includes bibliographical references and index.
  ISBN 978-1-60413-307-3 (hardcover : alk. paper)
  1. United States. President (1861–1865 : Lincoln). Emancipation Proclamation—
Juvenile literature. 2. Slaves—Emancipation—United States—Juvenile literature.
3. Lincoln, Abraham, 1809–1865—Juvenile literature. 4. United States—Politics and
government—1861–1865—Juvenile literature. 5. United States—History—Civil War,
1861–1865—Juvenile literature. I. Title. II. Series.
  E453.W86 2009
  973.7'14—dc22   2008030742

Chelsea House books are available at special discounts when purchased in bulk quantities for businesses, associations, institutions, or sales promotions. Please call our Special Sales Department in New York at (212) 967-8800 or (800) 322-8755.

You can find Chelsea House on the World Wide Web at http://www.chelseahouse.com

Series design by Erik Lindstrom
Cover design by Ben Peterson

Printed in the United States of America

Bang NMSG 10 9 8 7 6 5 4 3 2 1

This book is printed on acid-free paper.

All links and Web addresses were checked and verified to be correct at the time of publication. Because of the dynamic nature of the Web, some addresses and links may have changed since publication and may no longer be valid.

CONTENTS

1 The Importance of the Emancipation Proclamation   **1**

2 Forcing the Issue   **11**

3 Creating the Emancipation Proclamation   **25**

4 Political Fallout of the Proclamation   **39**

5 Reactions Around the World to the Proclamation   **52**

6 The Proclamation Changes the War's Course   **63**

7 The Thirteenth Amendment   **76**

8 The Proclamation's Legacy   **87**

Chronology and Timeline   **100**

Notes   **102**

Bibliography   **106**

Further Reading   **111**

Index   **113**

The Importance of the Emancipation Proclamation

The Emancipation Proclamation was the single most important document in ending slavery in America. It did not exist in a vacuum, however, and it did not end slavery by itself. Many things led up to it, and many things followed it.

One of the most important milestones on the road leading to the Emancipation Proclamation was reached on February 27, 1860. That evening, a tall, thin lawyer from Illinois named Abraham Lincoln made a speech in New York City.

At the time, Lincoln was relatively unknown. He only had limited experience when it came to politics. On the national level, he had served only a single term in Congress. But Lincoln was a rising star. He was well known as a strong voice against the most troublesome political issue of the day: slavery.

For decades, the individual states that made up America had been bitterly divided on this volatile question. Slavery was an integral part of life in the southern states. Should it be banned entirely? Or should it be allowed to continue in the South? And what of new territories and states entering the nation—should they be allowed to enforce slavery?

"THE SAME TYRANNICAL PRINCIPLE"

Lincoln's views on slavery were well known: he had been against it for many years. In 1854 he had stated, "Slavery is founded on the selfishness of man's nature—opposition to it on his love of justice." Lincoln had continued to establish his strong anti-slavery credentials while serving a term as a congressman from Illinois, and later while he was running for a Senate seat.

Lincoln lost that senatorial contest, but he became a celebrity through his eloquent appearances in debates with his opponent, Stephen Douglas. In one of these now-famous debates, Lincoln stated that slavery was "the issue that will continue in this country when these poor tongues of Judge Douglas and myself shall be silent." He went on:

> It is the eternal struggle between these two principles—right and wrong—throughout the world. . . . The one is the common right of humanity, and the other the divine right of kings. . . . It is the same spirit that says, 'You work and toil and earn bread, and I'll eat it.'
>
> No matter what shape it comes, whether from the mouth of a king who seeks to bestride the people of his own nation and live by the fruit of their labor, or from one race of men as an apology for enslaving another race, it is the same tyrannical principle.[1]

A MODERATE

As the public learned during these debates, Lincoln was not a polished politician. He was extremely tall, and he was so thin

A self-taught lawyer and U.S. congressman, Abraham Lincoln became well known for his moderate anti-slavery views. Although he believed slavery was evil in all respects and wanted to limit its existence in the United States, Lincoln was willing to work with Southern states to establish a gradual end to slavery.

that he seemed gaunt. He had an unsophisticated manner; a high-pitched voice; two huge, rough hands; and an awkwardly flat-footed gait.

But Lincoln also was personable, intelligent, and perceptive. Furthermore, he showed a willingness to work with others to find compromises. These characteristics brought him to prominence in a new political party: the Republicans. The Republican Party had been formed on a strongly anti-slavery platform. Some of its members, known as Radical Republicans, were strong abolitionists; they favored the immediate and complete end of slavery throughout the country.

Lincoln was not a radical; he was more moderate in his position. He hated slavery, was happy it was outlawed in the northern states, and was firmly opposed to letting it spread to new territories and states in the West. But his attitude was more conciliatory toward the South, where slavery was already established.

"A MORAL, SOCIAL, AND POLITICAL EVIL"

Lincoln did not believe that the immediate and total end of slavery would be the best solution for the South or for the country as a whole. He was in favor of gradual emancipation. He thought this would be best for everyone, including slave owners—who would have been deprived of what was, legally, their property—and the slaves themselves—who would not have been prepared for freedom in a nation that overwhelmingly considered them inferior creatures.

Lincoln also was a strict constitutionalist. This meant that he believed in closely following the laws set forth in the U.S. Constitution. And Lincoln did not believe that the Constitution, as it was then written, gave the federal government the right to end slavery. Writer Frank Donovan notes,

> Lincoln abhorred slavery, but not with the fanaticism of the abolitionist. He called slavery 'a moral, social, and political

evil,' but he did not accept the view, held only by extreme radicals in that day, of complete equality between the races. This was not based on a feeling of Negro inferiority. Rather, complete equality was impossible under the conditions which prevailed at that time. Like Thomas Jefferson, he hated slavery, but he did not know what to do about it in practical, political, or humanitarian terms.[2]

A VISIT EAST

Lincoln's moderate views appealed to many in the Republican Party. He was considered a long-shot candidate for the Republican nominee for president of the United States in the elections of 1860. His visit to the east in February therefore was an important milestone in his rising career.

New York City was especially important. It was the biggest metropolis in the nation, with the largest concentration of influential newspapers. New York also was the home of the leading contender for the Republican presidential nominee, Senator William H. Seward.

Lincoln's visit thus held the promise of major attention from Republican powers. Historians Philip B. Kunhardt Jr., Philip B. Kunhardt III, and Peter W. Kunhardt write: "This was his chance to demonstrate the quality of his mind and his style to the Eastern leaders who were needed to support any real run for the top office."[3]

Travel in those days was cumbersome, and the route from Lincoln's home in Springfield, Illinois, to New York City was not swift. Lincoln had to take five trains, over the course of three days, to reach his destination. When he finally arrived, the Illinois lawyer learned that the venue for his public address had changed.

Lincoln had been scheduled to speak at Plymouth Church in Brooklyn, one of the city's boroughs. Plymouth was the home church of a famous anti-slavery minister, Henry Ward Beecher. But a change in venue brought Lincoln to the larger and more prestigious Cooper Institute (since renamed Cooper Union) in Manhattan, the heart of the city.

THE COOPER UNION SPEECH

Lincoln's Cooper Union speech was lengthy—more than 7,000 words—and took more than an hour to deliver. In fact, it was one of the longest speeches Lincoln would ever make; generally he was known for the concision and brevity of his public addresses.

Despite its length, the speech was not rambling. It was closely reasoned and persuasive. Lincoln delivered it in plain language, not in the flowery, bombastic, pompous style that was common then. Powerfully and convincingly, he argued that America's founding fathers, the statesmen who had created the Constitution, had wanted Congress to regulate slavery—even though many of them were slave owners.

Lincoln had spent months painstakingly researching his facts, using them to find clear patterns and to reach a rational conclusion. William Herndon, Lincoln's law partner in Illinois, was not at Cooper Union that night, but he was familiar with the text of the speech. Herndon later wrote: "It was constructed with a view to accuracy of statement, simplicity of language, and unity of thought. In some respects like a lawyer's brief, it was logical, temperate in tone, powerful—irresistibly driving conviction home to men's reasons and their souls."[4]

"BETTER THAN WE"

In the course of his speech, Lincoln specifically named the 21 signers of the Constitution (out of a total of 39) who, as states-men, later had voted to regulate slavery by banning its spread to new territories. Among them was the nation's first president, George Washington, who signed a law regulating slavery in just this way. Lincoln concluded that the federal government still had the right to control slavery in new territories.

Lincoln then drew parallels between the Founding Fathers and the situation as it stood in 1860:

I do not mean to say we are bound to follow implicitly in whatever our fathers did. To do so, would be to discard all the lights of current experience—to reject all progress—all improvement. What I do say is, that if we would supplant the opinions and policy of our fathers in any case, we should do so upon evidence so conclusive, and argument so clear, that even their great authority, fairly considered and weighed, cannot stand; and most surely not in a case whereof we ourselves declare they understood the question better than we.[5]

"LET US HAVE FAITH"

Lincoln also quoted one of the most famous founding fathers, Thomas Jefferson. Jefferson was an advocate of gradual emancipation, as well as deportation of former slaves to a country of their own. He had written: "It is still in our power to direct emancipation, and deportation, peaceably, and in such slow degrees, as the evil will wear off insensibly; and their places be, *pari passu* [equally, fairly], filled up by free white laborers. If, on the contrary, it is left to force itself on, human nature must shudder at the prospect held up."[6]

Lincoln added to this his own belief that the federal government had the right to control the spread of slavery but not its continuation in states that already had it. He stated:

Mr. Jefferson did not mean to say, nor do I, that the power of emancipation is in the Federal Government. He spoke of Virginia; and, as to the power of emancipation, I speak of the slaveholding States only. The Federal Government, however, as we insist, has the power of restraining the extension of the institution—the power to insure that a slave insurrection [revolt] shall never occur on any American soil which is now free from slavery.

Lincoln ended his lengthy address by urging his fellow Republicans to do the right thing. He said, "Let us have faith that right makes might, and in that faith, let us, to the end, dare to do our duty as we understand it."[7]

ON THE ROAD

The audience at Cooper Union—1,500 politically minded New Yorkers—received Lincoln's speech with great enthusiasm. In fact, one reason he was at the podium for over an hour was that the audience repeatedly interrupted him with cheering and applause.

Lincoln's stirring speech and warm reception were major news. The next day, most of New York City's many newspapers published the text of his speech. The distinguished *New York Times* deemed it front-page news.

Among the people in the audience that night was Horace Greeley, the editor of one of New York's most prominent antislavery newspapers, the New York *Tribune.* The influential Greeley was enthusiastic about Lincoln. He commented in his paper, "No man ever before made such an impression on his first appeal to a New York audience."[8]

Lincoln soon gained important support beyond New York as well. He spoke in several other eastern cities to equally fervent audiences before returning home. His words also were widely reprinted as campaign literature.

ON TO THE WHITE HOUSE

Lincoln's moving speech at Cooper Union did much to put him firmly on the road to the White House. In Chicago that

(*opposite*) In his electrifying speech at Cooper Union, Lincoln encouraged the Republicans to work with the Democrats, despite their opposing views on slavery. Although his speech greatly impressed his New York audience, secessionists threatened to leave the Union if Lincoln were elected president. Lincoln won entirely on the strength of his support in the North, and South Carolina became the first state to secede from the Union.

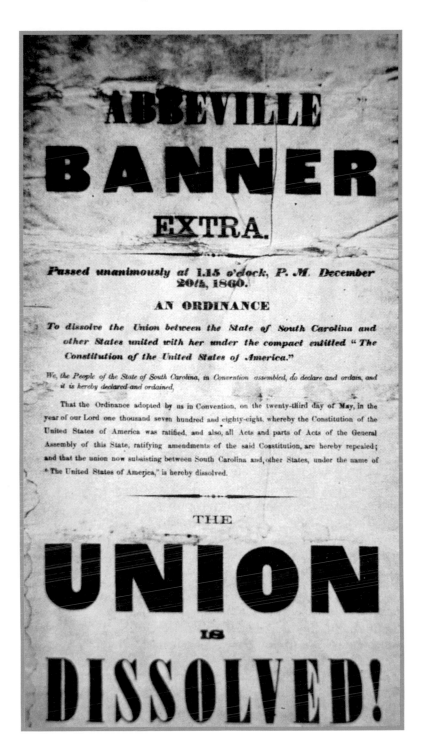

summer, the Republicans held their convention to nominate a candidate. It was not an easy decision. The most prominent contenders, including Seward and Salmon P. Chase, Ohio's governor, were considered unlikely to win a general election. Their abolitionist positions were considered too radical.

The nomination went to a moderate instead—Abraham Lincoln. His Democratic opponent was his old senatorial rival, Stephen Douglas. (Meanwhile, Southern Democrats nominated their own candidate, the pro-slavery John Cabell Breckinridge.) Running for vice president with Lincoln was another strong abolitionist, Hannibal Hamlin.

The election was held that November. Lincoln was soundly hated throughout the South, but he had many supporters in the North. He won the contest without the support of a single Southern state.

IN THE WAKE OF THE ELECTION

Lincoln's rise to the nation's highest office caused an immediate uproar. Many of the Southern states responded by seceding from the Union—a drastic action that led to the start of the Civil War. This war would last for years, and its end, among other things, would signal the end of slavery in America.

The speech Lincoln made at Cooper Union was a crucial link in this chain of events leading to emancipation. It made him nationally prominent and led directly to his nomination. Without it, he may never have become president. And if Lincoln had not become president, the story of slavery in America might have been very different. This story began much earlier; its roots stretch back to more than 200 years before Lincoln was elected president, to the time when slaves first arrived.

Forcing the Issue

No one knows exactly how many African people, in total, became part of the slave trade to North America. Estimates vary widely, from 10 million to 100 million. Of these, only a small number, perhaps 10 percent, arrived in the 13 English colonies that eventually became the United States.

The first recorded slaves in the colonies landed in 1619. By 1750, there were about 200,000 of them. Most were in the South, where a massive amount of manual work was needed to produce labor-intensive crops such as rice, tobacco, sugarcane, and eventually cotton.

After the colonies achieved independence from England in 1776, the practice of slavery continued to vary depending on the individual state. The northern states generally shunned it, and slowly they banned the practice. By 1804, slavery was abolished in all of the northern states.

"NATURALLY INFERIOR"

However, slavery continued to be a central part of life in the South, and the federal government tolerated its presence there. Four of the first five presidents were southerners, and all of them were slave owners—although, to varying degrees, they all deplored the practice and hoped to see it end. George Washington noted, "There is not a man living who wishes more sincerely than I do to see a plan adopted for the abolition of it."[1]

By 1860, although only one-fourth of whites in the South owned slaves, the number of slaves toiling there was up to roughly 4 million, and their presence had become crucial to the South's economy. They were considered private property, with no more rights than a cow or a horse might have. Owners were free to buy and sell slaves, and the slaves lived in the worst imaginable conditions and were routinely subjected to cruelty and degradation. Slaves were frequently beaten, raped, or separated from their families. In some cases, owners could kill slaves without fear of serious reprisal.

Slave revolts were a constant fear for owners. To lessen the chance of rebellion, owners typically forbade slaves to possess weapons or to meet with other slaves. They could not testify against white people in court, and they typically received far harsher punishments for crimes than whites did. Nor were they able to receive an education; in some regions, it was illegal for a white person to teach a slave to read.

Southern whites had little trouble justifying this state of affairs. Their belief—bolstered with religious scriptures and pseudoscientific claims—was that whites were inherently superior in intelligence, talent, and moral standards. The Scottish philosopher David Hume was typical of many when he wrote in 1748: "I am apt to suspect the Negroes and in general all the other species of men to be naturally inferior to the whites. There never was a civilized nation of any other complexion than white."[2]

Men and women, mostly from Africa, were brought to the United States during the colonial period and were seen as property. Public slave auctions were frequent events where landowners could purchase slaves to join their workforce. Families were frequently separated at these markets, as fathers, mothers, and children were sold off to whoever would pay the highest price for them.

FREEDOM OF SORTS

It was different in the North. Many whites there actively opposed slavery. African Americans there, called "free Negroes," could not be owned. Even so, free Negroes did not have easy lives. The bitter lesson was that freedom was not the same as equality.

Blacks still were not citizens in northern states, and thus they were denied such basic rights as voting. The races also remained mostly segregated. The best hotels, restaurants, theaters, and other public places were off-limits to African Americans; those that did cater to them were shabby and inadequate. Education was a rarity, and usually only the most menial jobs were available.

Still, freedom in the North clearly was superior to slavery in the South. If possible, therefore, slaves saved money to buy their freedom and go north. But this was difficult, and in desperation slaves occasionally rebelled against their masters. One such rebel was Nat Turner, a deeply religious Virginian. In 1831, he led others in a revolt that killed over 50 whites before Turner was captured and hung.

Some slaves simply tried to escape. The most common route to the North was a dangerous secret itinerary called the Underground Railroad. Free blacks and sympathetic whites provided slaves with food, shelter, transportation, and clothing along this route. One of the most famous of these supporters was Harriet Tubman, who was born a slave but found her freedom in the North. Tubman risked certain death by traveling to and from the South some 19 times, successfully leading a total of at least 300 slaves to freedom.

SCOTT, STOWE, AND BROWN

A handful of African Americans tried to use the legal system to gain their freedom. One pioneer in this effort was Dred Scott. Scott argued in court that he had become a free man when he traveled with his owner from their home in the slave state of Missouri to the free states of Illinois and Minnesota.

In 1852, however, the Missouri Supreme Court ruled against Scott. It decided that he had become a slave again by reentering Missouri. The case went to the U.S. Supreme Court, which again decided against Scott. In 1857, it ruled that no black person, free or enslaved, could be an American citizen; therefore, no black person had the right to sue in federal court. The court ruled that black people were "so far inferior that they had no rights which the white man was bound to respect."[3]

Meanwhile, a number of northern whites worked tirelessly to abolish slavery throughout the nation. Many used speeches and books as their primary weapons. One especially influential book was Harriet Beecher Stowe's novel *Uncle Tom's Cabin*, a best seller from 1852 that poignantly highlighted the plight of slaves.

Other abolitionists preferred direct action. One was John Brown, a white man obsessed with the belief that only violence would free the slaves. Brown's zeal was remarkable; the distinguished African-American leader Frederick Douglass once noted that Brown was "as deeply interested in our cause, as though his own soul had been pierced with the iron of slavery."[4] But Brown's dream of starting a race war, which he hoped would lead to the establishment of a state run by ex-slaves, ended in 1859. He was captured while raiding a government arsenal and was hung for treason.

CIVIL WAR

By 1860 the always-delicate political balance between slave states and non-slave states was near collapse. Lincoln's election that year tipped the balance, causing several states to secede and form the Confederate States of America.

The first, South Carolina, seceded immediately after Lincoln's election, two months before he even took office. The stated reason was the election of a president "whose opinions and purposes are hostile to slavery."[5]

By February 1861, six more states had joined South Carolina: Mississippi, Florida, Alabama, Louisiana, Georgia, and Texas. Tensions continued to mount; Lincoln swore to keep the nation together by any means necessary. Violence seemed inevitable.

It came in April 1861 when Southern troops, on orders from Confederate president Jefferson Davis, fired on Union (Northern) troops occupying Fort Sumter in South Carolina. The Union troops were forced to surrender. Lincoln ordered the recapture of Sumter, as well as other forts and customs houses that Confederate forces were claiming.

The attack on Fort Sumter marked the official start of the Civil War. No one, especially in the North, expected it to last long. Writing of the man who was once Lincoln's rival and who was now his secretary of state, historian William K. Klingaman comments, "Seward predicted that the Union would win in sixty or ninety days. Lincoln was less optimistic."[6]

SEEKING ASYLUM

Indeed, the Confederate cause gained ground as the year wore on. There was more armed conflict, including several major battles. Four more states—Virginia, Arkansas, North Carolina, and Tennessee—joined the rebellion. The Confederates also claimed portions of territories that today are Oklahoma, New Mexico, and Arizona. Meanwhile, several states between the North and the South were slave states but remained loyal to the Union.

As the bloody war dragged on, some military leaders in the North sought to weaken the South's resources, depriving it of material and manpower by confiscating private Confederate property—including slaves. This practice of seizing the South's human property started with General Benjamin F. Butler, who at this point was in charge of Fort Monroe in Virginia.

Butler declared that slaves in his territory were to be considered contraband—property that could be legally confiscated. Word spread quickly, and within three days nearly 60 slaves had sought protection at Fort Monroe. Angry owners insisted that the slaves be returned, but Butler refused. He sent them to work at the fort and telegraphed the War Department for clarification: "Are these men, women, and children, slaves? Are they free? . . . What has been the effect of the rebellion and a state of war upon [their] status?"[7]

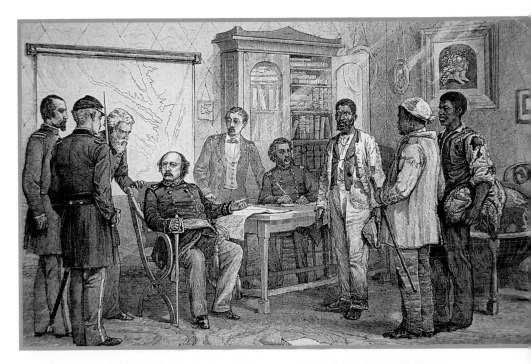

After General Benjamin Butler (*seated, left*) declared all slaves in his territory to be free, slaves in the area flocked to his base, Fort Monroe, for protection. Inspired by Butler's action, other Union generals made similar announcements.

BUTLER AND FRÉMONT

Lincoln had always been clear in his conviction that he had no immediate plans to interfere with slavery in the South. In his first inaugural address he had stated: "I have no purpose, directly or indirectly, to interfere with the institution of slavery in the States where it exists."[8] The president still believed that, and he believed that Butler's actions were unconstitutional. Nonetheless, he did not officially reprimand the general and took no action against him.

Several other Union generals followed Butler's lead. Soon, scores of slaves were running away and traveling to Union forts, looking for protection and asking to be declared as contraband.

One of the military leaders was General John C. Frémont, commander of the Union Army in Missouri. Frémont proclaimed that all slaves owned by actively rebelling Confederates in his territory were free: "The property . . . of all persons in the State of Missouri who shall take up arms against the United States, and who shall be directly proven to have taken active part with their enemies in the field, is declared to be confiscated to the public use; and their slaves, if any they have, are hereby declared free."[9]

This was too much for Lincoln, who declared, "I cannot assume this reckless position. Can it be pretended that it is any longer the government of the U.S.—any government of Constitution and law—wherein a General, or a President, may make permanent rules of property by proclamation?"[10] When Frémont refused to bend, Lincoln replaced him with the more conservative general Henry Halleck. Halleck immediately issued an order forbidding runaway slaves from seeking protection by the Union Army.

THE CONFISCATION ACTS

Meanwhile, the U.S. Congress was working on the Confiscation Acts. These acts were legislation designed to formalize the seizing of property belonging to Confederates—including slaves. The idea was to deprive the Confederate Army of as much slave labor as possible. Historian Edna Greene Medford comments, "Congress dared to do something about Confederate use of its slave labor force" by passing measures "designed to legalize what General Butler had already implemented at Fortress Monroe."[11]

The Second Confiscation Act, approved by Congress in July 1862, stated that, after a 60-day grace period, the slaves of Confederate sympathizers could be emancipated. Union army officers were forbidden to return runaways to their owners. The acts also established a compensation scheme to pay slave owners for their former property, and it set aside money to establish colonies outside the United States for former slaves.

Lincoln objected to the acts. His main concern was practical and political. He feared that the legislation might push the "loyal border states," especially Kentucky and Missouri, to join the rebels. After the president's objections were overridden, he asked the border states to accept the new legislation in good faith. He told a contingent of congressmen, "How much better for you, and for your people, to take the step which, at once, shortens the war, and secures substantial compensation for that which is sure to be wholly lost in any other event."[12]

As Lincoln feared, most politicians in the border states rejected the plan for compensated emancipation. Representative William H. Wadsworth of Kentucky stormed, "I reject it now; I utterly spit at it and despise it. Emancipation in the cotton States is simply an absurdity. . . . There is not enough power in the world to compel it to be done."[13]

EMANCIPATION AS A WAR MEASURE

The scorn raised by the Confiscation Acts seemed to be a major turning point for Lincoln. He sadly commented, "I was as nearly inconsolable as I could be and live."[14] He now began to consider something else.

The outlook for the North was bleak during the summer of 1862. Its war efforts were going poorly, its economy was faltering, and national bankruptcy was a real possibility. Public support for Lincoln's cautious moderation was dropping, and it was time, many felt, for drastic action. Governor Richard Yates of Illinois spoke for many when he said, "Blows must be struck at the vital parts of the rebellion."[15]

And so Lincoln began to deeply consider an idea that had been in the air for some time. Previously, he had stated repeatedly that the war was to restore the Union, not to end slavery. And he still believed that the Constitution prevented him from freeing the slaves as a domestic measure.

Now, however, he began to seriously contemplate emancipation as a war measure. Ending slavery, he reasoned, might turn the tide of the war. And it could be legally justified if it was a necessary military move.

Lincoln reasoned that emancipation would hurt the Confederacy in two key ways. It would deprive the South of vitally needed manpower. It also would change the moral tone of the war, thus altering the relationship between the Confederacy and the two leading powers of Europe—France and England.

This was important because these two countries could have continued to supply the South with desperately needed arms and ships. But France and England also were strongly anti-slavery. Lincoln hoped that abolition would end their support of the Confederacy.

"A SNAKE IN A BED"

Lincoln remained cautious. He still believed that the blame for slavery lay in both the North and the South, and he was able to see two sides to the issue. Historian Allen C. Guelzo comments that "prudence demanded that he balance the integrity of *ends* (the elimination of slavery) with the integrity of *means* (his oath to uphold the Constitution and his near-religious reverence for the rule of law)."[16]

Lincoln knew that achieving emancipation would both help and hurt. Using, as he often did, a down-to-earth comparison, the president remarked that slavery was like "a snake in a bed where children were sleeping. Would I do right to strike . . . there? I might hurt the children."[17]

Many commentators supported the president's cautious approach. For example, the influential magazine *Harper's Weekly* noted that Lincoln was "a leader whose moral perceptions are blinded neither by sophistry [misleading persuasion] nor enthusiasm—who knows that permanent results must grow, and can not be prematurely seized."[18]

Others urged quicker action, feeling that emancipation was necessary for victory. Thomas Wentworth Higginson, a prominent minister, soldier, and abolitionist, stated that "the idea of conquering rebellion without destroying slavery is only to be equaled by the idea of storming hell without disturbing the personal comfort of the devil."[19]

"MY PARAMOUNT OBJECT"

Another voice was that of newspaper editor Horace Greeley, who wrote an open letter to Lincoln in his New York *Tribune*. Greeley criticized Lincoln for not making slavery the primary issue of the war, and he accused him of putting political motives above moral principles.

Lincoln responded to Greeley by writing an open letter of his own. It emphasized the president's practical nature. He wrote:

> My paramount object in this struggle is to save the Union, and is not either to save or to destroy slavery. If I could save the Union without freeing *any* slave, I would do it; and if I could save it by freeing *all* the slaves, I would do it; and if I could save it by freeing some and leaving others alone I would also do that. What I do about slavery, and the colored race, I do because I believe it helps to save the Union.[20]

He knew that many Northerners opposed a "war for the Negroes," and that the majority supported containing slavery in the South and preventing its spread. He also expected fierce opposition from Democratic politicians, especially the pro-slavery and anti-war Copperhead Democrats. (The name apparently came from the deadly copperhead snake, which strikes without warning.)

Meanwhile Lincoln continued to worry about the border states. Historian William K. Klingaman writes, "The president feared that emancipation would shatter the northern consensus

(continues on page 24)

THE WRONGS OF SLAVERY

Lincoln's basic philosophy regarding slavery was well formed long before he became president. He frequently spoke of his belief that Northerners were just as much to blame for the wrongs of slavery as were Southerners. He also strongly believed that the institution was deeply ingrained in American life and would be difficult to erase.

Nonetheless, he was dead set against it. As early as the 1850s, he considered whether it might be better to leave the United States if pro-slavery forces succeeded in making the entire nation a slave-holding country. He wrote to a friend in 1855, complete with his own eccentric spelling and punctuation:

> Our progress in degeneracy appears to me to be pretty rapid. As a nation, we began by declaring that '*all men are created equal.*' We now practically read it, 'all men are created equal, *except negroes.*' Soon enough it will read 'all men are created equal, except negroes, *and foreigners and Catholics.*' When it comes to this I should prefer emigrating to some country where they make no pretense of loving liberty—to Russia, for instance, where despotism can be taken pure, and without the base alloy of hypocracy [sic].*

Shortly before Lincoln issued his Emancipation Proclamation, newspaper editor Horace Greeley published an open letter to the president in August 1862 that laid out his concerns over Lincoln's caution in treating the question of slavery:

> I do not intrude to tell you—for you must know already—that a great proportion of those who triumphed in your election, and of all who desire the unqualified suppression of the Rebellion now desolating our country, are sorely disappointed and deeply pained by the policy you seem to be pursuing with regard to the slaves of the Rebels. I write only to set succinctly and

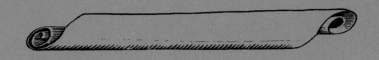

unmistakably before you what we require, what we think we have a right to expect, and of what we complain. . . .

We think you are unduly influenced by the counsels, the representations, the menaces, of certain fossil politicians hailing from the Border States. . . ."**

In July 1862, Congress and Lincoln approved the Second Confiscation Act. This act was designed to liberate slaves held in the rebel states and was essentially a precursor to the Emancipation Proclamation.

For "any person [who would] incite, set on foot, assist, or engage in any rebellion or insurrection against the authority of the United States, or the laws thereof," it stipulated imprisonment for up to 10 years, fines of up to $10,000, and liberation of their slaves. It also stated:

> All slaves of persons who shall hereafter be engaged in rebellion against the government of the United States, or who shall in any way give aid or comfort thereto, escaping from such persons and taking refuge within the lines of the army; and all slaves captured from such persons or deserted by them and coming under the control of the government of the United States; and all slaves of such person found on [or] being within any place occupied by rebel forces and afterwards occupied by the forces of the United States, shall be deemed captives of war, and shall be forever free of their servitude, and not again held as slaves.***

*Richard Striner, Father Abraham: Lincoln's Relentless Struggle to End Slavery, New York, N.Y.: Oxford University Press, 2006, p. 7.
**Henry Ketcham, The Life of Abraham Lincoln, Whitefish, Mont.: Kessinger Publishing, 2003, p. 142.
***"The Second Confiscation Act," July 17, 1862. Available online at http://www.history.umd.edu/Freedmen/conact2.htm.

(continued from page 21)

in favor of a war to preserve the nation, and might alienate the border slave states that remained in the Union—possibly leading them to secede and join the Confederacy."[21]

A NECESSARY STEP

Increasingly, Lincoln was beginning to see emancipation as a necessary step if he were to save the Union. In the end, he decided that the war emergency justified extraordinary measures. He later said, "Things had gone on from bad to worse, until I felt that we had reached the end of our rope on the plan of operation we had been pursuing; that we had about played our last card, and must change our tactics, or lose the game."

And so he began the difficult, painstaking task of writing the Emancipation Proclamation.

Creating the Emancipation Proclamation

One morning in June 1862, Lincoln went to the telegraph room of the War Department, where he received all his telegrams. He liked to work there because it was quiet compared to the hubbub and distractions of the White House. The president asked Captain Thomas T. Eckert, the officer in charge of the department, for a sheet of paper so he could write "something special."

Lincoln then sat down at the captain's desk and alternated between looking out the window and putting pen to paper. Eckert later wrote: "He did not write much at once. He would study [think] between times and when he had made up his mind he would put down a line or two, and then sit quiet a few minutes. After a time he would resume his writing."[1]

When the president was done for the day, he asked Eckert to lock the paper in a desk and keep it secret. Lincoln returned periodically all through that summer to work on the mystery document. Other matters often distracted him, but what he was working on in private was never far from his thoughts.

A WAR MEASURE

Lincoln's secret project, of course, was a first draft of the Emancipation Proclamation. It actually was the first of two parts. Today, this document is called the Preliminary Emancipation Proclamation.

Lincoln envisioned this first part essentially as a warning. He wanted to serve notice to the Confederacy that he would issue a full Emancipation Proclamation if the states in rebellion did not return to the Union. The president wanted to send a clear message: Come back—or your slaves will be freed.

Before he began writing, Lincoln had wanted to be certain that he was within his legal rights to emancipate the slaves, even as a form of war power. He therefore consulted William Whiting, the War Department's chief solicitor, or lawyer.

It was Whiting's opinion that the federal government would indeed be within its legal rights to free the slaves. Lincoln could use his position as commander in chief of the Army and Navy to declare emancipation a "necessary war measure." It would be considered a temporary emergency measure—not a law passed by Congress, but an order from the commander in chief. Such orders are specifically allowed under Article II, Section 2 of the Constitution.

Whiting's opinion satisfied Lincoln's doubts about the proclamation's legality. The president then visited the telegraph office and began assembling his thoughts. Over the summer of 1862, he continued to revise and refine them.

He prepared his dramatic pronouncement alone and without consulting his usual advisers. In fact, he worked without their knowledge. "Things had gone from bad to worse, until I felt we had reached the end of our rope," he later wrote. "I now determined upon the adoption of the emancipation policy;

As the war went on, Lincoln's views on gradual emancipation changed as he began to favor complete and immediate freedom for the enslaved people of the South. He prepared the Emancipation Proclamation, a document that shifted the focus of the war from restoring the Union to ending slavery. *Above*, Lincoln drafting the Emancipation Proclamation in the telegraph office of the White House.

and, without consultation with, or the knowledge of the Cabinet, I prepared the original draft of the proclamation."[2]

REFINING HIS THOUGHTS

Lincoln gave no indication to anyone of his plan. Publicly, he continued to promote his scheme of gradual compensated emancipation—a plan that would not have completely freed the slaves until 1900. Privately, however, his mind had firmly changed. Historian Doris Kearns Goodwin writes: "While Washington sweltered through the long, hot summer, Lincoln made the momentous decision on emancipation that would define both his presidency and the course of the Civil War."[3]

Meanwhile, a variety of abolitionist groups visited the White House. The president used these guests as foils for his own thinking by playing devil's advocate—that is, essentially agreeing with them but debating with them, trying to find flaws in their positions. Historian David Herbert Donald writes:

> Lincoln . . . often played a kind of game with the numerous visitors who descended on him to urge him to free the slaves. The measures they advocated were precisely those that he was attempting to formulate in his document at the War Department. If he challenged their arguments, he was, in effect, testing his own.[4]

By mid-June, Lincoln was ready to share the draft of his proclamation with a few trusted others. Probably the first to hear it was his vice president, Hannibal Hamlin. On June 18, Lincoln and Hamlin rode horses at the Soldiers' Home, a veterans' retirement home about three miles from Washington, D.C. The Lincolns had a small cottage there that they often used to escape the heat of the city.

After their ride, Lincoln and Hamlin ate dinner and the president read a draft of the preliminary pronouncement to his colleague. The president asked for criticism and Hamlin, long an advocate of emancipation, replied, "There is no criticism to be made."[5] However, at Lincoln's urging, he did offer suggestions for minor revisions.

READING IT TO THE CABINET

Lincoln continued to revise the document, and in July he read it to two other trusted colleagues, Secretary of State William H. Seward and Secretary of the Navy Gideon Welles. He planned to raise the issue during a regularly scheduled cabinet meeting in his office on July 21 (the simple fact that Lincoln called his cabinet together was a sign that something important was

Copyright 1876 by Currier & Ives N.Y   GIDEON WELLES, Sec.of the Navy   MONTGOMERY BLAIR, P.M.Genl   CALEB B. SMITH, Sec.of the Interior
PRESIDENT LINCOLN.   SALMON P. CHASE, Sec.of the Treasury.   WILLIAM H. SEWARD, Sec.of State   EDWARD BATES, Atty.Genl   EDWIN M. STANTON, Sec.of War.

PRESIDENT LINCOLN AND HIS CABINET.

IN COUNCIL, SEPT.22ND 1862. ADOPTING THE EMANCIPATION PROCLAMATION, ISSUED JANY. 1ST 1863.

New York. Published by Currier & Ives. 125 Nassau St.

After Lincoln completed the Emancipation Proclamation, he gathered his advisers together to hear their opinions on the matter. Though most were in favor of abolishing slavery, others had reservations or opposed the measure. Above is a depiction of Lincoln and his cabinet adopting the proclamation in 1863.

happening; he usually preferred to meet with them individually), but Lincoln spent most of this meeting on other issues and did not get to his main purpose. The next day, July 22, the president called another meeting.

Goodwin writes: "There, surrounded by evidence of the ever-expanding war, with battlefield maps everywhere—rolled in standing racks, placed in folios on the floor, and reclining up against the walls—the conversation from the previous day continued."[6]

Lincoln read the proclamation to the assembled secretaries, pausing occasionally to explain specific passages. By the usual standard of Lincoln's writing, it was extremely dull. Many of his famous speeches, including the Cooper Union speech and especially the Gettysburg Address (which he would deliver in November 1863), are emotional and inspiring. In this case, however, Lincoln created a rational and logical text that carefully avoided inflammatory language. Historian William K. Klingaman notes that it was a "calm, reasoned document [that] contained no outrage or condemnation of slavery, no call for a moral crusade."[7]

WHAT IT SAID

This language was very deliberate. Lincoln wanted to make sure that his writing would be legally invincible, so that it would stand up in the court battles that were sure to come. It therefore had to be precise, dispassionate, and logical. Guelzo comments, "The Proclamation is a legal document, and legal documents cannot afford very much in the way of flourishes. They have work to do. . . . Lincoln could afford eloquence at Gettysburg; he could not in the Proclamation."[8]

Its first paragraph reconfirmed Lincoln's goal of keeping the Union whole. It spoke of "the constitutional relation between the United States, and each of the states, and the people thereof, in which that relation is, or may be suspended, or disturbed."[9]

In the second paragraph, Lincoln reiterated his proposal for compensated emancipation. He made it clear that he hoped Congress would provide funds to any Confederate state that agreed to return to the Union and to begin emancipating its slaves. By making this offer, Lincoln protected himself from a charge of illegally violating constitutional property rights.

The second paragraph also contained a promise to continue efforts to resettle former slaves in a new colony, perhaps

(continues on page 33)

THE PRELIMINARY EMANCIPATION PROCLAMATION

It has often been noted that two of the most important documents in American history are written in the dry, careful language of a lawyer. Lincoln wrote both the Preliminary and Secondary Emancipation Proclamations knowing that they might be challenged in court, and he wanted to make sure they would stand up. This excerpt is from the Preliminary Emancipation Proclamation, issued by Lincoln on September 22, 1862:

> By the President of the United States of America,
> A PROCLAMATION
>   I, Abraham Lincoln, President of the United States of America, and Commander-in-Chief of the Army and Navy thereof, do hereby proclaim and declare that hereafter, as heretofore, the war will be prosecuted for the object of practically restoring the constitutional relation between the United States, and each of the States, and the people thereof, in which States that relation is, or may be, suspended or disturbed.
>   That it is my purpose, upon the next meeting of Congress to again recommend the adoption of a practical measure tendering pecuniary aid to the free acceptance or rejection of all slave-States, so called, the people whereof may not then be in rebellion against the United States and which States may then have voluntarily adopted, or thereafter may voluntarily adopt, immediate or gradual abolishment of slavery within their respective limits; and that the effort to colonize persons of African descent, with their consent upon this continent, or elsewhere, with the previously obtained consent of the Governments existing there, will be continued.

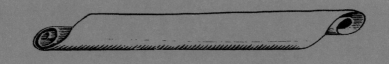

Another excerpt from the Preliminary Proclamation:

And be it further enacted, That all slaves of persons who shall hereafter be engaged in rebellion against the government of the United States, or who shall in any way give aid or comfort thereto, escaping from such persons and taking refuge within the lines of the army; and all slaves captured from such persons or deserted by them and coming under the control of the government of the United States; and all slaves of such persons found on [or] being within any place occupied by rebel forces and afterwards occupied by the forces of the United States, shall be deemed captives of war, and shall be forever free of their servitude and not again held as slaves.

And I do hereby enjoin upon and order all persons engaged in the military and naval service of the United States to observe, obey, and enforce, within their respective spheres of service, the act, and sections above recited.

And the executive will in due time recommend that all citizens of the United States who shall have remained loyal thereto throughout the rebellion, shall (upon the restoration of the constitutional relation between the United States, and their respective States, and people, if that relation shall have been suspended or disturbed) be compensated for all losses by acts of the United States, including the loss of slaves.

In witness whereof, I have hereunto set my hand, and caused the seal of the United States to be affixed.

(continues)

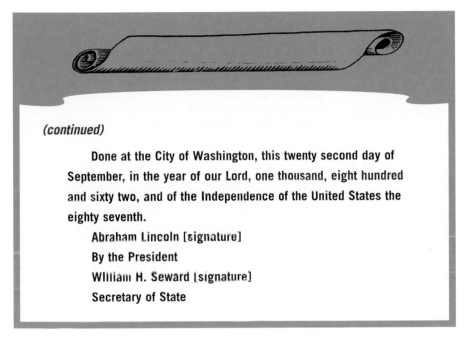

(continued)

Done at the City of Washington, this twenty second day of September, in the year of our Lord, one thousand, eight hundred and sixty two, and of the Independence of the United States the eighty seventh.

Abraham Lincoln [signature]

By the President

William H. Seward [signature]

Secretary of State

(continued from page 30)

on another continent. This was designed to placate the many whites, Northern and Southern, who feared the presence of large numbers of free blacks around them. Lincoln also argued that the freed slaves would benefit economically and politically from colonizing their own land.

REST OF THE DOCUMENT

Lincoln did not use the word *freedom* until he reached the proclamation's third paragraph. The president dropped this bombshell using the same dry, lawyerlike language he used throughout the rest of the document. He wrote, "All persons as slaves within any state, or designated part of a state, the people whereof shall be in rebellion against the United States shall be then, thenceforward, and forever free"[10] as of January 1, 1863.

Lincoln went on to promise that, as long as he was president, "the executive government of the United States, including the military and naval authorities thereof, will . . . recognize such persons as being free."[11]

The document also cited legal and political precedents for its existence. In particular, it mentioned the Second Confiscation Act and the article of war that Congress had passed in March 1862, prohibiting U.S. military personnel from returning runaway slaves. The proclamation ended with an order to all Union military officials to fulfill their duties under the Second Confiscation Act and with a reiteration of Lincoln's promise to compensate former slave owners.

MIXED REACTIONS

When Lincoln finished reading the statement, members of his cabinet expressed their opinions. Secretary of State Seward, a lifelong abolitionist, heartily supported it. The secretary of war, Edwin M. Stanton, also approved. Stanton recognized the document for what it was—an excellent military measure that could well turn the tide for the North.

Salmon P. Chase, the treasury secretary, was another ardent abolitionist, and he approved of the proclamation in spirit. He worried, however, about its long-term effects. Chase argued that there was "great danger" in freeing all of the slaves at once and that such a measure could lead to "depredation and massacre on the one hand, and support to . . . insurrection [slave revolt] on the other."[12] He favored letting the army organize and arm slaves district by district, as individual generals saw fit.

Not everyone was as positive. For example, the postmaster general, Montgomery Blair, worried about the political fallout for the Republican Party. He foresaw great losses in the upcoming congressional elections. Blair also worried that the army would resist the proclamation and that the border states might secede.

The attorney general, Edward Bates, gave the measure only halfhearted support. A conservative, Bates opposed slavery but also opposed complete emancipation, and he predicted disaster unless the colonization of ex-slaves was certain. And Interior Secretary Caleb B. Smith threatened to resign, though this did not upset Lincoln.

"THE WORDS FINALLY WENT IN!"

The president made it clear that he had read the proclamation to the cabinet because he wanted their advice on its style, not its substance. He was determined to follow through with it, no matter how they felt. Lincoln therefore asked them to give him only suggestions for minor political and literary refinements.

As a result, the document was somewhat altered. For example, Seward argued that it should be strengthened by adding a commitment from the federal government to maintain the freedom of ex-slaves, even after the Lincoln administration ended. Lincoln felt that this was impractical, but, he later recalled, "Seward insisted that we ought to take this ground; and the words finally went in."[13]

Also, conservative cabinet members convinced Lincoln to drop a passage stating that the government would not repress former slaves in any efforts toward freedom. The members were worried that these words were inflammatory. The fear was that they could be interpreted as meaning that the Union would support slave rebellions.

Another change involved Lincoln's cautious reservations about admitting African-American men into the Union Army. He was not sure that blacks and whites were ready to fight side by side. However, the radical Republicans in his cabinet persuaded him to add a clause stating that former slaves would be welcome as soldiers.

Seward also asked Lincoln to add a phrase making it clear that colonization would take place only if the ex-slaves consented. The president and the entire cabinet agreed to this amendment.

DELAYING

Lincoln put stock in one man's opinion more than any other in his cabinet. This man was Seward. The president listened carefully to Seward's strongly worded suggestion that he delay announcing the proclamation.

In Seward's opinion, the timing of the proclamation was crucial. It needed to come after a major victory for the North. Seward argued that if a plan for emancipation had been made public at the beginning of the war, it would have been seen as a moral act.

He pointed out, though, that the Union Army now was in retreat everywhere. If emancipation were to be announced immediately, Lincoln's critics would accuse him of admitting weakness. The proclamation would be seen as "the last measure of an exhausted government, a cry for help . . . our last shriek, on the retreat."[14]

Lincoln accepted Seward's advice. He agreed to set the measure aside and to wait for a Union victory. This opportunity came in September, in the wake of the bloody Battle of Antietam, also called the Battle of Sharpsburg.

ANTIETAM

Antietam, which took place in Maryland, was the war's first major battle to take place on Union soil. It also was the costliest single day of fighting in American history—some 23,000 men were killed, wounded, or missing after just one day of fighting. (For comparison: This figure is more than all the American casualties in the Revolutionary War, War of 1812, Mexican War, and Spanish-American War put together.)

Antietam was not an unqualified victory for the Union. The battle's outcome was inconclusive, and the overly cautious tactics of the commanding Northern general, George B. McClellan, came under severe scrutiny and criticism.

However, in the short term it was a success in one important way. Union forces were able to stop the Confederate general Robert E. Lee in his first attempt to invade the North.

Even more crucial was the long-term result. The battle was enough of a victory that Lincoln had his opportunity to issue the Emancipation Proclamation. As a result, Antietam became a significant turning point in the Civil War. The New York

The battle at Antietam was the first attempted Confederate invasion of the North and one of the bloodiest battles in U.S. history. Though there was no overwhelming victor, Lincoln used the battle as an opportunity to announce the Emancipation Proclamation and the abolishment of slavery in the United States.

Times noted, "At last our Generals in the field seem to have risen to the grandeur of the National crisis. Sept. 17, 1862, will, we predict, hereafter be looked upon as an epoch in the history of the rebellion, from which will date the inauguration of its downfall."[15]

ISSUING THE PRELIMINARY PROCLAMATION

Lincoln continued to make minor changes to the proclamation, and he finished a final draft in his cottage at the Soldiers' Home. Then, on September 22, 1862, just five days after the battle of Antietam, he made it public.

Lincoln later remarked on the speed of the action at this point. He commented, "I finished writing the second draft of the preliminary proclamation, came up [to Washington, D.C.] on Saturday, called the Cabinet together to hear it, and it was published the following Monday."[16]

The reaction to it was just as swift.

Political Fallout of the Proclamation

Roughly 100 days elapsed between Lincoln's announcement of the Preliminary Emancipation Proclamation and January 1, 1863—the deadline he set for the second announcement. Naturally, during that time the country gave enormous attention to the news and to its possible outcome. Spirited debates took place everywhere—in newspapers, government offices, public meeting places, and private homes. Some people rejoiced, while some seethed.

AN IMPERFECT DOCUMENT

Even for those who had prayed for an end to slavery, Lincoln's Preliminary Proclamation hardly was a complete solution. In many ways, it was severely limited.

For one thing, the Union had no real way to enforce the proclamation in rebel states. The measure did not, by itself, have the power to physically free anyone. (It did, however, make it clear that no one in the South would be allowed to stop slaves from potentially reaching freedom. It also promised that no U.S. civilian or military official would take action to hinder them.)

Another shortcoming was that the document exempted the border states from freeing their slaves; these slaves amounted to about one-quarter of the total. This was because Lincoln still needed the loyalty of the border states and could not risk angering them. Seward noted the bitter irony: "We show our sympathy with slavery by emancipating slaves where we cannot reach them and holding them in bondage where we can set them free."[1]

Furthermore, the success of the proclamation depended on the support of Congress and the federal courts. Support from Congress was likely, since the Republicans were in the majority. But the courts still could overturn the decree. And there was a very real possibility that the courts, ruling that emancipation was strictly a wartime measure, would overturn it when the conflict ended.

LINCOLN'S MESSAGE TO CONGRESS

The president was fully aware that the proclamation was, by itself, not a complete solution. Still, he felt that it was an important beginning. This was evident in his annual message to Congress, which was delivered on December 1, 1862. In this speech, Lincoln reiterated his plan for compensated emancipation, and he urged lawmakers to adopt a constitutional amendment making it a reality.

In the speech, the president explored many other aspects of abolition. He looked at the economic, cultural, financial, constitutional, and ethical effects it could have, and how it might finally be reached. Lincoln concluded his message with these ringing words:

> Fellow-citizens, we cannot escape history. . . . The fiery trial
> through which we pass, will light us down, in honor or
> dishonor, to the latest generation. . . . In giving freedom to
> the slave, we assure freedom to the free—honorable alike in
> what we give, and what we preserve. We shall nobly save, or
> meanly lose, the last best hope of earth. . . . The way is plain,
> peaceful, generous, just—a way which, if followed, the world
> will forever applaud, and God must forever bless.[2]

By the end of December, the war still was dragging on. The
deadline the president had set for voluntary emancipation was
drawing close, and no Confederate states had returned to the
Union. It was time to deliver on the promise of the Preliminary
Proclamation.

LAST-MINUTE SUGGESTIONS

As he had with the first document, Lincoln wrote the Final
Proclamation himself, but he accepted suggestions for changes
from his cabinet. On the last three days of the year, the president convened them three times for this purpose.

At the first meeting, Lincoln read aloud a draft of the final
document, again written in his own hand, and asked for comments. Treasury Secretary Chase spoke up, objecting to language that exempted those portions of the Confederacy where
Union troops already were in control. To do so, he argued,
would be an administrative nightmare. But Lincoln replied
that the exemption was needed for constitutional reasons. The
proclamation was only a wartime measure. In those regions
that were not at war, the Constitution clearly prohibited him
from interfering with the property of citizens.

At the next day's meeting, Secretary of State Seward spoke
up. Lincoln had written that he wanted to "enjoin" all free
blacks to avoid violence. But Seward was worried about slave
uprisings, and he recommended strengthening the document's

language so that it would "command and require" rather than simply "enjoin."

Attorney General Bates also had suggestions. He wanted to include language to make it very clear that the proclamation was only a wartime measure. He also wanted to specifically state that former slaves would not be allowed in the Union Army.

Lincoln did not accept the suggestions of either Seward or Bates. However, at the third meeting the next day, he did agree to a few very minor changes in wording. These minor changes were the only ones that altered the president's text.

MAKING IT OFFICIAL

The morning of New Year's Day was bright and crisp in Washington, D.C. Lincoln attended the traditional White House reception and stayed until about 1:00 P.M. When the last guests left, he went to his office, upstairs in the East Wing of the White House. There he met Seward and Seward's son Fred, who was the assistant secretary of state. About a dozen other people joined them as well, but it was not a formal ceremony.

Lincoln sat down at a desk with the Emancipation Proclamation before him. Most of the text was written in the president's own hand, with a few exceptions. Two paragraphs had been taken verbatim from the Preliminary Proclamation, and so these had simply been clipped from a printed copy and pasted onto the draft of the final version. Also, a State Department clerk added a formal opening and closing to the document.

Just before signing, Lincoln said, "I never, in my life, felt more certain that I was doing right than I do in signing this paper."[3] The president then took up a gold pen and started to sign his name. However, his hand was shaking, and he had to set the pen down. He tried again after a moment, and again he had to stop.

At the time that Lincoln issued the Emancipation Proclamation, it was criticized for not going far enough. It gave Lincoln the executive power of freeing the slaves only in states still in rebellion. Therefore, in states that remained loyal to the Union slavery was still protected under the Constitution. Today the Emancipation Proclamation is regarded as one of the greatest documents in U.S. history.

His hand was shaking violently. Lincoln recalled later, "I could not for a moment control my arm. I paused, and a superstitious feeling came over me which made me hesitate. . . . In a moment I remembered that I had been shaking hands for hours with several hundred people, and hence [there was] a very simple explanation of the trembling and shaking of my arm."[4]

Then, having rested, the president confidently signed his name, smiled, and said, "That will do." Seward added his signature, and the Great Seal of the United States made the document official.

WHAT IT SAID

Like the preliminary edict about 100 days earlier, Lincoln's Final Proclamation began by acknowledging that it was solely the president's responsibility. It recalled his earlier warning that a second decree would be issued should the rebellion still be ongoing by the New Year.

Also like the Preliminary Proclamation, the document's heart was found several paragraphs into the text. "I do order and declare," Lincoln wrote, "that all persons held as slaves within said designated States, and parts of States, are, and henceforward shall be free; and that the Executive government of the United States, including the military and naval authorities thereof, will recognize and maintain the freedom of said persons."[5]

The Final Proclamation made clear how Lincoln intended to carry this out. He aimed to liberate any slaves who escaped from their masters. He wrote: "All the slaves of persons who shall hereafter be engaged in rebellion against the Government of the United States . . . escaping . . . and taking refuge within the lines of the army, and all slaves captured from [rebels] or deserted by them . . . shall be deemed captives of war, and shall be forever free of their servitude, and not again held as slaves."[6]

Lincoln also made it clear that he was not advocating slave rebellion, instead "enjoining" (urging) freed slaves to abstain from violence except in cases of self-defense. The document further recommended to freed slaves that they find work for reasonable wages.

"SINCERELY BELIEVED TO BE AN ACT OF JUSTICE"

Lincoln also included language promising that the federal government would welcome ex slaves as soldiers with the Union Army. He stipulated, however, that this would be "to garrison forts, positions, stations, and other places, and to man vessels of all sorts in said service."[7] There was no mention in the document of arming ex-slaves for combat duty. There also was no mention of the president's plans, outlined in the Preliminary Proclamation, regarding compensation and colonization.

Like the Preliminary Proclamation, the Final Proclamation limited freedom only to those slaves in regions of the Confederacy that were still under direct Confederate control. This meant that slaves in the border states—Maryland, Delaware, Missouri, and Kentucky—still were not affected. Slaves in the parts of the Confederacy that the Union Army controlled—which by then included Tennessee, parts of Virginia and Georgia, the new state of West Virginia, and the city of New Orleans and its surrounding parishes (districts)—also were not included in the proclamation.

The document's language, for the most part, was as dry as that of the first proclamation. Lincoln again was careful to use language that would protect the decree from future court challenges. At the end of the proclamation, however, Lincoln did insert one sentence that betrayed the emotion and eloquence more characteristic of his speechmaking. He wrote: "And upon this act, sincerely believed to be an act of justice . . . I invoke the considerate judgment of mankind, and the gracious favor of Almighty God."[8]

SENDING THE NEWS OUT

On the evening of New Year's Day, Lincoln walked to the telegraph office at the War Department. He wanted to hear the latest news from Tennessee, where General William Rosecrans was battling a Confederate force at Stones River. Lincoln also wanted to watch as word of the Final Proclamation went out by telegraph.

The president told the soldiers in the office stories about his days as an Illinois lawyer and otherwise chatted as the operators prepared to send the text out. At about 8:00 P.M., transmission of the Final Proclamation began.

Millions of people had been eagerly awaiting this news. There were vigils in many northern cities by groups of free blacks and white abolitionists. Many people also put candles in their windows as symbols of freedom. Virtually every black church in the North was filled by midnight with congregations singing and praying together.

In Washington, D.C., a large group gathered in front of the White House to congratulate Lincoln. When the president appeared at a window, the crowd cheered. Lincoln bowed but did not go out into the crowd.

"IT WAS INDEED A TIME OF TIMES"

Elsewhere in the nation's capital, an African-American minister, the Reverend Henry M. Turner, waited with a large crowd, both black and white, at the offices of the *Evening Star* newspaper. (Earlier, Washington, D.C. had passed a law abolishing slavery within its limits, so these were free blacks.) When the new edition of the paper appeared, Turner tore out the page reprinting the Emancipation Proclamation and ran down Pennsylvania Avenue, waving it over his head.

As he reached his church, nearly a mile away from the newspaper office, the crowd waiting there saw him coming and raised a deafening cheer. Turner tried to read the proclamation aloud but was so out of breath that another man had to finish the job. The minister recalled:

> Every kind of demonstration and gesticulation was going on. Men squealed, women fainted, dogs barked, white and colored people shook hands, songs were sung, and by this time cannons began to fire at the navy-yard. . . . It was indeed a time of times. Nothing like it will ever be seen again in this life. . . . The first day of January 1863, is destined to form one of the most memorable epochs in the history of the world.[9]

MORE REACTIONS

Elsewhere in the country were similar scenes, as groups waited eagerly in churches or newspaper offices for news via telegraph. Word of the proclamation started arriving in many cities shortly before midnight on New Year's Day and spread quickly. Groups of ecstatic abolitionists wept, shouted, embraced one another, and sang hymns.

In Boston, Massachusetts—long the center of the abolitionist movement—there also was rejoicing. One huge gathering was at the Music Hall, where an orchestra played in celebration and participants included poet Henry Wadsworth Longfellow, writer Harriet Beecher Stowe, and philosopher Ralph Waldo Emerson. At the Tremont Temple, a black Baptist church, a crowd celebrated with speeches and singing all night long—moving to another church after midnight. One of those present, Frederick Douglass, called it a "worthy celebration of the first step on the part of the nation in its departure from the thralldom [tyranny] of the ages."[10]

Among ordinary black people, the proclamation met with wide rejoicing and praise. This is perhaps best summarized by the words of Hannah Johnson, a free African-American freedwoman from Buffalo, New York. Johnson's son served in the

54th Regiment, New York Infantry. Soon after the proclamation was made public, she wrote to Lincoln: "They tell me, some do, you will take back the Proclamation, don't do it. When you are dead and in Heaven, in a thousand years that action of yours will make the Angels sing your praises."[11]

FREDERICK DOUGLASS
(1818–1895)

Champion of Equal Rights

Frederick Douglass was born Frederick Augustus Washington Bailey as a slave in Talbot County, Maryland, in 1818. As an infant, he was taken away from his mother and lived with his grandmother until he was moved to the Wye House plantation, where he was given to Hugh Auld in Baltimore. There he was secretly taught the alphabet by Auld's wife, Sophia, until Hugh forbade this instruction. Douglass continued to teach himself to read by using books belonging to Sophia's son. At 13, he read a collection of political essays and speeches called *The Columbian Orator*, which he credited with defining his views on human rights and the injustice of slavery.

Douglass was sent to live with Thomas Auld and then on to Edward Covey, a slave breaker (someone who specialized in breaking the spirits of rebellious slaves). In his memoirs, *Narrative of the Life of Frederick Douglass*, he described this time as the turning point in his life as a slave. After being beaten nearly every day for six months, Douglass had had enough and wrestled Covey to a draw in a fight. Covey never attempted to beat him again. Douglass said that day he became a man.

Several times Douglass tried to escape his various owners but had no success. Finally, on September 3, 1838, carrying identification papers given to him by a free black man, Douglass successfully escaped by boarding a train going from Baltimore to New York dressed as a sailor back from sea duty.

AT CAMP SAXTON

Away from the North's urban centers, such as on Georgia's Sea Islands, the celebrations were equally fervent. The Union had occupied these remote islands since the early part of the war. The white population had left for the mainland and the black

He moved on to New Bedford, Massachusetts, and joined the abolitionist movement. After telling his life story, he was encouraged to become a full-time lecturer. He traveled throughout the North to recruit members to the American Anti-Slavery Society. He soon became the leading black abolitionist and speaker, and he continued to work for civil rights for the remainder of his life.

New Year's Day 1863 was one of great rejoicing for the abolitionist activists of the country, as they gathered to await word via telegraph that Lincoln was making good on his promise. Frederick Douglass, who had been critical of Lincoln in the past for being too cautious, recalled waiting with a crowd of others in his memoirs:

Eight, nine, ten o'clock came and went, and still no word. . . .
At last, when patience was well-nigh exhausted . . . a man (I think it was Judge Russell) with hasty step advanced through the crowd, and with a face fairly illuminated with the news he bore, exclaimed in tones that thrilled all hearts, 'It is coming! It is on the wires!' . . . My old friend Rue, a colored preacher, a man of wonderful vocal power . . . led all voices in the anthem, 'Sound the loud timbrel O'er Egypt's dark sea, Jehovah hath triumphed, his people are free.'*

* Striner, p. 186.

Groups of African Americans and abolitionists waited patiently through the evening on January 1, 1863, to hear news of Lincoln's Emancipation Proclamation. *Above*, **the 1st South Carolina Colored Volunteer Regiment, the first black military unit created in the South by the Union, rejoice after hearing the announcement of the proclamation.**

population had stayed, although the slaves' lives were much as they had been before the war, since the white owners and their families often stayed on the mainland for long periods to avoid malaria.

But their lives began to change dramatically after word of the proclamation arrived. Charlotte Forten, an African-American schoolteacher and activist on the Sea Islands, recalled that New Year's Day for her was the greatest day in her country's history.

That day, Forten took a group of her students by ferry to Camp Saxton, the headquarters of the 1st South Carolina Colored Volunteers, the first regular black regiment in the United

States Army. (It had been organized recently by runaway slaves.) Forten recalled:

> There was an eager, wondering crowd of the freed people in their holiday attire, with the gayest of head-handkerchiefs, the whitest of aprons, and the happiest of faces. The band was playing, the flags streaming, everybody talking merrily and feeling strangely happy.... Long before we reached Camp Saxton we could see the beautiful grove. Some companies of the First Regiment were already drawn up in parade formation—a fine soldierly-looking set of men.[12]

"FREEDOM WAS SURELY BORN"

A military chaplain read the proclamation aloud to the cheering crowd. Forten recalled that some sang "My Country, 'Tis of Thee" and thrilled the crowd. Uniformed (but unarmed) black soldiers marched and maneuvered. Forten wrote, "To us it seemed strange as a miracle—this black regiment, the first mustered into the service of the United States, doing itself honor in the sight of the officers of other regiments, many of whom, doubtless, came to scoff."[13]

Heading home, the schoolteacher recalled, "Our hearts were filled with an exceeding great gladness, for although the Government had left much undone, we knew that Freedom was surely born in our land that day."[14]

But there was, indeed, much left undone. Announcing the Emancipation Proclamation was only a first step. The political fallout of Lincoln's declaration—as well as the hard work of enforcing it—was yet to come.

Reactions Around the World to the Proclamation

The entire country soon was aware that the Emancipation Proclamation was being made public and going into effect. Most of the Northern dailies printed the text of the document on January 2, 1863. Newspaper editors and other observers quickly weighed in with their opinions.

Typical of liberal Northern papers was the *New York Times*, which called the proclamation the most far-reaching document ever issued by the government and asserted that its wisdom was unquestionable and its necessity indisputable. The paper further declared that the Emancipation Proclamation would spawn "a revolution . . . It changes entirely the relations of the National Government to the institution of Slavery. Hitherto Slavery has been under the protection of the Government; henceforth it is under its ban."[1]

Another prominent paper, the strongly abolitionist New York *Tribune*, made the feelings of its editor, Horace Greeley, even plainer. A headline in that paper trumpeted: "God Bless Abraham Lincoln!"[2]

THE MILITARY REACTS

The Union Army distributed 15,000 copies of Lincoln's declaration to its troops. Some high-ranking Union officers were furious. They were conservatives who had never favored emancipation and were outraged at the prospect of "fighting for slaves." But many other officers, especially those in midlevel positions, supported the move as a sound military measure.

Opinions among the regular soldiers were similarly mixed. While many approved of the measure, many more did not. Lincoln replied to them that he hoped they could see fit to fight just for their country. He said, "You say you will not fight to free Negroes. Some of them seem willing to fight for you; but, no matter. Fight you then, exclusively, to save the Union. I issued the proclamation on purpose to aid you in saving the Union."[3]

Many observers, even those sympathetic to the plight of the slaves, were dismayed. They feared that the Emancipation Proclamation's publication dashed all hopes of a quick end to the war. They assumed that the challenge laid down by Lincoln would lead to a sharp increase in Southern volunteers and a boost in morale for the Confederacy. The South would be more determined than ever to succeed in breaking away. To those with antiwar feelings, a compromise and a cease-fire were no longer serious possibilities.

This was stated by a number of prominent voices on both sides of the conflict. Union General Henry Halleck sadly remarked, "There is now no possible hope of reconciliation. We must conquer the rebels or be conquered by them."[4] And, in his annual statement to the Confederate Congress in January

Union soldiers and officers soon found out about Lincoln's new war strategy, as copies of the Emancipation Proclamation were printed and distributed among the troops. Although the document received mixed reactions, the men continued to fight in order to preserve the Union. *Above*, Union soldiers in Fredricksburg, Virginia.

1863, President Jefferson Davis asserted that "a restitution of the Union has been rendered forever impossible by the adoption of a measure which . . . neither admits of retraction nor can coexist with union."[5]

"WE SHOUT FOR JOY"

Reaction among Northern politicians was mixed. Some, primarily Democrats, spoke out against the proclamation, typically stating their opinions that it was likely to drag the war out indefinitely. However, most Republicans were favorable toward it. Some even tried to pass a law through Congress that would have freed Southern slaves by legal statute. However, Lincoln vetoed this bill. He did not feel that the North had the right to emancipate the slaves simply by passing an ordinary statute.

GIDEON WELLES
(1802–1878)

Secretary of the Navy

Gideon Welles was Lincoln's Secretary of the Navy. Welles, a passionate abolitionist, was one of the first people to hear Lincoln read his draft of the Preliminary Emancipation Proclamation. Welles had been active in the Republican Party before joining Lincoln's cabinet, but he was more conservative than many others in the party. After Lincoln's death, he changed his affiliation to the Democrats. He noted in his diary on the day of the announcement:

> The Emancipation Proclamation is published in this evening's *Star*. This is a broad step, and will be a landmark in history. The immediate effect will not be all its friends anticipate or its opponents apprehend. . . . The character of the country is in many respects undergoing a transformation. This must be obvious to all and I am content to await the results of passing events, deep as they may plough their furrows in our once happy land. This great upheaval which is shaking our civil fabric was perhaps necessary to overthrow and subdue the mass of wrong and error which no trivial measure could eradicate. The seed which is being sown will germinate and bear fruit, and tares [weedy plants] and weeds will also spring up under the new dispensation.

As might be expected, abolitionists and pro-abolition newspapers generally rejoiced at the news. Even some radical abolitionists who had criticized Lincoln in the past for being too cautious applauded the announcement. One of these was William Lloyd Garrison, the editor of the influential anti-slavery newspaper *The Liberator.* Garrison grandly wrote that the Emancipation Proclamation was "a great historic event, sublime in its magnitude, momentous and beneficent in its far-reaching consequences."[6]

THE DRAFT RIOT

Many ordinary people in the North were incensed at the prospect of slaves gaining their freedom. Large numbers of Northern whites, especially recent immigrant groups, were fearful that ex-slaves would migrate north and compete for their jobs. Tension between blacks and whites over job competition led to riots in a number of cities, among them Cincinnati, Chicago, Detroit, Philadelphia, Boston, and Newark.

The worst of these was the New York City Draft Riot. It broke out in July 1863, initially in reaction to the government's decision to create a draft to bring hundreds of thousands of young men into the Union Army. Most of the estimated 50,000 rioters were Irish immigrants, though the mob included many German immigrants and others as well.

The violence began as a protest against the draft but soon focused on the city's black population, and African Americans, especially men, became scapegoats for the rioters' frustrations. The immigrants already were competing with free blacks for work—usually the lowest-paying menial jobs—and they resented the idea that they might be forced to fight for the freedom of millions more coming from the South.

The violent Draft Riot resulted in the murders of 11 black people, including 1 who was attacked by a crowd with clubs and paving stones, then hung from a tree and burned. Three hundred people were left homeless, and countless were injured.

Already concerned over the influx of ex-slaves in the competitive labor market, the white working class in New York City became enraged about the creation of a draft for the Union Army. Riots of mostly German and Irish immigrants raged through the city, their anger directed toward any blacks they came across on the street. An orphanage housing black children was also destroyed in the frenzy.

Property destruction also was widespread, including dozens of homes, the offices of the New York *Tribune*, and an orphanage for black children.

The worst of the violence lasted for four days. It finally ended when Lincoln sent regiments of militia and volunteer troops in to control the city. These troops restored order and remained camped around the city for several weeks until tensions died down.

SOUTHERN REACTIONS

In the South, a few slaves expressed reluctance about the Emancipation Proclamation as the prospect sank in of leaving the only lives they had ever known. Overall, however, the reaction among Southern African Americans was one of rejoicing. This was typified by the comments of a bilingual newspaper in New Orleans, *L'Union*, which had been started by free blacks. The newspaper exulted:

> Let us all be imbued with these noble sentiments which characterize all civilized people.... Let us be resolute. Let us rise up in all the majesty and with the charity befitting Christians, let us preach by example to all men, so that they will follow the road which leads to liberty.... Down with the craven behavior of bondage! Stand up under the noble flag of the Union and declare yourselves hardy champions of the right.[7]

Of course, the reaction among pro-slavery whites was far from enthusiastic. Confederate President Jefferson Davis told his Congress that the proclamation could have "but one of three possible consequences—the extermination of the slaves, the exile of the whole white population of the Confederacy, or the absolute and total separation of these states from the United States."[8]

This feeling was echoed among soldiers and ordinary citizens as well. One Confederate soldier, First Lieutenant Charles Colcock Jones Jr., of Georgia, wrote to his father that Lincoln's proclamation was "the crowning act of the series of black and diabolical transactions which have marked the entire course of his administration. I look upon it as a direct bid for insurrection, as a most infamous attempt to incite flight, murder, and rapine on the part of our slave population."[9]

Virtually every Southern newspaper editor agreed with these sentiments. The Richmond (Virginia) *Whig*, for example, denounced the "fiend's new program," calling it "a dash of the pen to destroy . . . our property." Another Richmond paper, *The Examiner*, condemned it as "the most startling political crime ... yet known in American history" and assured readers that its "sole purpose" was to incite slave rebellion.[10] And a third Richmond paper, *The Enquirer*, feared that slave riots were a certainty and stated that Lincoln was thus condemning the Southern Confederacy to dire destruction.

EUROPEAN REACTIONS

Overseas, the Emancipation Proclamation had the effect that Lincoln had hoped for. He had anticipated that it would cast the war, in foreign eyes, in a moral light—that is, as a war to end slavery. Since few nations wanted to be publicly seen as condoning slavery, foreign governments would be reluctant to officially recognize the Confederacy as a separate and legitimate nation.

And Europe was overwhelmingly anti-slavery. Giuseppe Garibaldi, a prominent Italian political and military leader, said that Lincoln was "the heir of the aspirations of John Brown."[11] One of the fathers of communism, Karl Marx, approved of the basic idea behind the proclamation, although he complained that it did not go far enough and that its dry language reminded him of "ordinary summonses sent by one lawyer to another on the opposing side."[12]

America's ambassador to Spain, Carl Schurz, wrote home to say, "It is my profound conviction that as soon as the war becomes distinctly one for and against slavery, public opinion [in Europe] will be so strongly, so overwhelmingly in our favor that, in spite of commercial interests or secret spites, no European government will dare to place itself, by declaration or act, upon the side of a universally condemned institution."[13]

The most important of these foreign countries for the South, militarily and politically, were Great Britain and France. The British government and the government of the emperor, Louis Napoleon, in France had been generally sympathetic to the Confederate States of America. Of these two, Great Britain was the most crucial.

The Emancipation Proclamation was well received in various European nations, most of which were vehemently opposed to slavery. As was Lincoln's intention, the abolishment of slavery deterred foreign countries from providing aid to the Confederacy in the Civil War. *Above*, audience members in Exeter Hall in England celebrate after hearing the declaration of freedom.

"THE ENEMY'S CATTLE"

This was, in large part, for economic reasons. Great Britain needed supplies of cotton from the South for its textile mills. The British textile industry employed roughly a fifth of the nation's factory workers, and supplies of raw cotton from the American South were vital to keeping these workers employed.

The Confederacy, in return, was counting on European support in the form of arms, supplies, and warships. Some of this aid had already taken place. Before Lincoln's announcement, for example, Great Britain already had built several warships for the South, including the CSS *Florida* and the CSS *Alabama.*

The need for support from Europe became so crucial that Confederate President Davis even considered issuing his own proclamation to free the slaves. This was in desperate hope of wooing British and French support. Davis's idea, however, was bitterly opposed by Southern slave owners and never progressed far.

Some Britons were skeptical and cynical about the news of the Emancipation Proclamation. A few newspapers there argued that the measure was arrogant, had no legal force, and indicated weakness. The London *Spectator* had editorialized in October 1862, soon after the Preliminary Proclamation was issued: "The [Union] government liberates the enemy's slaves as it would the enemy's cattle, simply to weaken them in the . . . conflict. . . . The principle is not that a human being cannot justly own another, but that he cannot own him unless he is loyal to the United States."[14]

"A GREAT POPULAR MOVEMENT"

But this feeling was a minority opinion. The majority of Britons applauded the proclamation—not for economic reasons but for moral ones. This is illustrated by a meeting of abolitionists that took place late in January 1863 in Exeter Hall, London. So many showed up that two further meetings had to be scheduled to accommodate the overflow crowds.

Journalist Henry Adams, the son and secretary of America's ambassador to England, noted this wave of approval among ordinary English men and women. After attending a large meeting of workers in the industrial city of Manchester, Adams reported, "The cry was 'Emancipation and reunion.' . . . Every allusion [reference] to the South was followed by groaning, hisses and howls, and the enthusiasm for Lincoln and for everything connected with the North was immense."[15] Adams also wrote to his brother Charles:

The Emancipation Proclamation has done more for us here [in England] than all our former victories and all our diplomacy. It is creating an almost convulsive reaction in our favor all over this country. . . . Certain it is that public opinion is deeply stirred here and finds expression in meetings, addresses to President Lincoln, deputations to us, and standing committees to agitate the subject and to affect opinion, and all the other symptoms of a great popular movement.[16]

A WARTIME ELECTION

The Emancipation Proclamation had a major effect on politics at home as well. It had been an important factor in the 1862 election cycle. The Democrats, who were generally antiemancipation, had made some significant gains then, including 28 seats in the House of Representatives and the important governorship of New York.

On the other hand, Lincoln's support within the Republican Party had been solidified by his actions. In the wake of the proclamation, his renomination in 1864 for a second term was cemented. In that wartime contest, Lincoln's Democratic opponent was his former top general, George B. McClellan. There also was a Radical Republican contender: John C. Frémont, another former Union Army general. In the election in November (in which only 24 states voted, since 11 had seceded), Lincoln was easily reelected.

The Emancipation Proclamation also gave the Union strength, in more than one way. It provided moral force for Lincoln's cause: the government of the North was no longer fighting simply to preserve the Union but also to right a moral wrong. And the proclamation had a dramatic impact on more concrete aspects of the war—aspects that would become very clear over the next months of battle.

The Proclamation Changes the War's Course

As news of the Emancipation Proclamation spread into the South, the lives of millions of people took dramatic new turns. Among the slave population of the South, the impact was, of course, stunning.

The biggest immediate impact was in the upper regions of the South—that is, in those regions that were closest to the border with the North. Increasingly, groups of slaves, hearing that they were set free, became "unfaithful" and left their masters.

Many ran away to Northern outposts in the South or to the North itself. In an effort to stop this, some slave owners in the regions closest to the borders sold their slaves to other whites living further in the interior. Other owners simply moved themselves and their slaves further into the Deep South.

THE SLAVES LEAVE THEIR MASTERS

A handful of slaves, especially those living in remote regions far from the borders, chose to remain loyal to their masters. Historians cite several reasons for this. For one thing, they might have been reluctant to leave the only homes they had ever known for a frightening new life of freedom. They may have had genuine affection for their masters' families. Or they may have feared the very real threat of execution by angry owners.

But these were exceptions to the rule. More typically, slaves on Southern plantations and farms grew increasingly bolder as Union troops—now on the offensive—steadily advanced on and commandeered these lands. There were very few instances of violent slave rebellion. Instead, slaves simply refused to work for their masters or to submit to punishment. As Union forces occupied their masters' land, the slaves often took an active role in seizing and distributing property, amid a general air of celebration.

The numbers of free slaves steadily grew larger. As the Union forces encroached further into rebel territory, thousands more slaves were freed each day.

A HUGE INFLUX OF NEW PEOPLE

The Union military already was aware of the issue of freed slaves, since the Confiscation Acts previously had given the military the task of confiscating "contraband" property in the form of runaway slaves. The influx of newly freed slaves created by the Emancipation Proclamation did not, therefore, constitute a new problem.

It did, however, create the new problem of scale. It was no longer a matter of a few runaway "guests" taking refuge in Union forts. Now thousands of new arrivals were coming every day to Union outposts, and they were no longer "contraband of war." They were free men and women.

When former slaves moved from the South to find freedom behind Union lines, the military officers were soon overwhelmed with providing food, shelter, and work for the newcomers. Many former slaves found jobs in the Union Army and were paid an army wage. *Above*, a former slave works as a mess corporal for the Union.

The enormous task of overseeing the care of these people was daunting. A number of Union officers, such as Chaplain John Eaton of the 27th Ohio Infantry Volunteers, were assigned to the job. Eaton and his colleagues did what they could. They set up camps and field hospitals for the former slaves, organized work groups around the Union camps, and set up training programs. They also devised ways to keep families together whenever possible, instead of splitting them up as slave owners routinely had done.

The numbers were overwhelming. By July 1864, a year and a half after the Emancipation Proclamation took effect, Eaton alone was supervising more than 110,000 former slaves. Many of them were earning their own keep as soldiers, scouts, laundresses, cooks, officers, servants, or laborers for the military. Others had found private employment, typically as mechanics, barbers, laborers, and the like.

THE CONFEDERACY FALTERS

The huge influx of ex-slaves looking for refuge in Northern outposts was a big drain on the Confederacy, and it powerfully affected the South's ability to maintain itself. Slaves had been an important part of the Confederate war machine, even though they had not served as soldiers—for the vast majority of white Southerners, the concept of arming black men, or even using them as unarmed soldiers, was out of the question.

Nonetheless, slaves were essential for other war-related tasks. For example, slaves on farms were needed to produce food and sew uniforms for the army. They produced the cotton that paid for arms and other war materials. They built and repaired roads for the military. They worked on fortifications and railways, and they labored in essential jobs in factories, shipping yards, hospitals, and mines. This let the South release white men for direct service in the Confederate forces.

All that changed dramatically when slaves began to leave their masters. The massive loss of manpower, in time, dealt a crushing blow to the Confederacy.

As the war dragged on, the South began to falter in other ways as well. For one thing, the Confederate government bureaucracy was inefficient and sluggish.

Infighting among various political factions within the Confederacy weakened it further. A major reason for this infighting centered on the question of the rights of states versus a more centralized government. The biggest problem was that many legislatures in Southern states refused to adequately pay to finance the Confederate military. They felt that this was intruding unfairly on the rights of individual states. Partly because of this, the South's military forces were in steady decline.

There were other reasons for this decline as well. The death toll in battles was horrifically high. Many soldiers deserted. Northern ships blockaded Southern ports, allowing only a trickle of desperately needed supplies through. And a number of crucial warships were lost, with no money left to replace them.

MORE PROBLEMS FOR THE CONFEDERACY

As many able-bodied Southern men as possible were sent into battle, and this had a devastating impact on the home front. It left few men available for nonmilitary labor such as farming. Old men, boys, women, and a shrinking number of slaves shouldered the burden instead.

Things continued to get worse for the South. A crushing blow came when the Confederacy lost all possibility of significant help from European powers. This had been basically guaranteed when the Emancipation Proclamation became effective, and it was cemented in the summer of 1863 by major Union victories at Gettysburg and Vicksburg. After these battles, the North clearly had the upper hand, and Europe was reluctant to support the South in any way.

Meanwhile, food production in the South was dropping, made worse by drought and military requisitions. There were protests and "bread riots" by mobs of citizens, mostly women. In Richmond, Virginia, the Confederate capital, thousands of protestors formed a gathering that covered 10 square blocks. It was mostly peaceful, but the protestors dispersed only when President Davis threatened to have his militia fire on them.

The South always had been adamantly opposed to the idea of using slaves as soldiers. But as casualties and desertions continued to deplete the rebel army, an increasingly desperate Confederacy began to contemplate the idea. In the spring of 1865, the Confederate Congress approved the recruitment of black infantry units and President Davis signed an act called the Negro Soldier Law.

However, the Confederacy did not guarantee the future freedom of any black volunteer. As a result, no more than 200 slaves agreed to become Confederate soldiers. None of them saw any battle action.

THE UNION ADMITS BLACK SOLDIERS

As the South was experiencing increasing difficulties, the fortunes of the Union forces were changing for the better. A significant reason for this was that, thanks to the Emancipation Proclamation, black men were allowed to become soldiers.

Since the beginning of the war, free blacks in the North had found work as civilian laborers for the armed forces. But they had not been regular soldiers. There still were significant opponents—including Lincoln—of using them as soldiers, much less to arming them and using them in combat.

The Emancipation Proclamation changed that. It specifically urged former slaves to enter "into the armed service of the United States to garrison forts, positions, stations, and other places, and to man vessels of all sorts in said service."[1]

Huge numbers of former slaves, eager to join, responded to the call. Among whites in the North, opinion gradually shifted and a groundswell of support grew in favor of training and arming black soldiers. In many cases, this was purely practical. Northerners could see that an infusion of new troops might well turn the tide of the war.

The prospect of black Union troops infuriated Southerners, who considered the practice barbaric and contrary to accepted

Although they were paid less than their white counterparts, many black people, including former slaves, joined the Union Army as soldiers, cooks, and guides. These black volunteers, which included Harriet Tubman and two of Frederick Douglass's sons, were dedicated to their cause and fought bravely in battles. At the end of the war, 16 black soldiers were given the Medal of Honor for their valor.

rules of war. Confederate President Davis proclaimed that any captured Union officers in charge of black troops would be treated as outlaws and executed as felons; black soldiers, meanwhile, would be sold into slavery. Lincoln retaliated by asserting that for every Union soldier executed as a felon (which would have been in violation of the accepted rules of war), a Confederate soldier would be killed.

Neither side carried out its threats, however, with perhaps one exception: an incident in April 1864 known as the Fort

Pillow Massacre. Controversy still exists over this incident, in which rebel forces captured Fort Pillow, a Union outpost in Tennessee. Contrary to the accepted rules of war, they may have executed a number of Union soldiers, mostly African American, after the soldiers had surrendered.

"A FIERCE ENERGY"

General David Hunter was the first Union military leader to take direct action concerning black soldiers. Even before the proclamation took effect, Hunter formed the nation's first all-black regiment, the 1st South Carolina (African Descent)

REACTIONS TO BLACK SOLDIERS IN THE UNION ARMY

Union Army general David Hunter was a strong advocate of arming and training African Americans for the military. In 1862, even before Lincoln issued his Emancipation Proclamation, Hunter formed the 1st South Carolina Volunteers (African Descent), the first Union Army regiment of black soldiers. At first, Lincoln ordered Hunter to disband this unit, but eventually Congress approved it.

Hunter also issued an unauthorized order that freed slaves in Georgia, South Carolina, and Florida—the Southern states that were under his control. Lincoln canceled this order, worrying that it might cause slave-holding border states to leave the Union, but it was significant nonetheless as a precursor to the Emancipation Proclamation.

Thomas Wentworth Higginson was a minister, soldier, and dedicated abolitionist. During the war, Higginson was a colonel in the 1st South Carolina Volunteers, the first authorized regiment of black soldiers. Higginson often commented on the pride he felt while commanding his troops: "I had been an abolitionist too long, and had

Regiment. This troop was made up of volunteer ex-slaves from the region of South Carolina that Hunter controlled.

A number of other Union commanders followed suit. Like Hunter, they were white officers in charge of black units. The troops they organized proved to be not only eager but brave and skilled. They put to rest white fears that ex-slaves might not be up to the task.

Colonel Thomas Wentworth Higginson, who was in charge of the 1st South Carolina Volunteers (the successor to Hunter's group), was a staunch supporter of black combat troops. He commented, "There is a fierce energy about them. . . . No

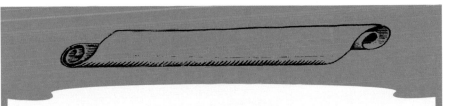

known and loved John Brown too well, not to feel a thrill of joy at last on finding myself in the position where he only wished to be."

After the war, Higginson remained devoted to the cause of equal rights for the races and genders. In particular, he championed such things as the preservation of African-American music.

John C. Frémont, who in 1856 had been the first candidate for president on the new Republican ticket, later became a general in the Union Army. In 1861, Frémont declared martial law in Missouri, confiscated the private property of secessionists, and emancipated the slaves there in a direct precursor to the Emancipation Proclamation.

Lincoln ordered Frémont to revise his order, since he worried that it would cause Missouri to join the South. When Frémont refused, Lincoln revoked the general's order and relieved him of his duties. Frémont later was placed in command of troops in Virginia, Tennessee, and Kentucky.

officer in this regiment now doubts that the key to the success-ful prosecution of this war lies in the unlimited employment of black troops."[2]

"VERY IMPORTANT, IF NOT INDISPENSABLE"

At first, Lincoln remained skeptical about the use of African-American troops. He worried that the races were too different, that black and white soldiers fighting side by side might be too volatile a mix.

Any doubts were erased from his mind by numerous reports of the skill and bravery of black soldiers in battle. Lin-coln came to agree with Higginson and others who supported black combat troops. He stated, "The colored population is the great *available* and yet *unavailed of*, force for restoring the Union."[3]

The president authorized the formation of a large-scale army of former slaves, coordinated by Senator Andrew John-son, who was then the military governor of Tennessee. Soon the North had such an influx of black soldiers that Lincoln created a separate department within the War Department devoted to them: the Bureau of Colored Troops.

Lincoln considered these new soldiers "very important, if not indispensable."[4] He further stated that he could never agree to letting them become slaves again. "I should be damned in time and eternity," he said, "for so doing."[5]

JOINING, NOT JOINING

In the two years between the Emancipation Proclamation taking effect and the end of the war, nearly 200,000 African-American men joined up. Roughly three-quarters of these were former slaves. They formed, among other groups, 6 regiments of the U.S. Colored Cavalry, 11 regiments and 4 companies of the U.S. Colored Heavy Artillery, 10 batteries of the U.S. Col-ored Light Artillery, and 100 regiments and 16 companies of the U.S. Colored Infantry.

Not all newly freed black men were eager to join the Union Army. There were several good reasons why they might have been reluctant. For one thing, black soldiers, no matter their rank, did not receive the same pay as their white counterparts. Until 1864, a black private earned $10 per month, as opposed to the $16.50 a white of equal rank received. Not until after the war did the government end this discrepancy in pay for white and black soldiers.

Several other factors discouraged potential black recruits. Among these were the North's refusal to commission black officers; the contempt many whites showed black soldiers; the draw of steady, noncombat employment in factories and elsewhere; disproportionate assignments to heavy labor and unwanted duty; and repeated Confederate threats to hang or sell into slavery any captured black soldiers.

THE WAR ENDS

The Emancipation Proclamation effectively broke the back of the Confederacy. The infusion of black soldiers into the Union Army gave the North an all-important edge in military force. The South, meanwhile, was stripped of a crucial supply of labor.

The South also lost any hope of backing from England and France. Thus, it was unable to manufacture or import enough ships, artillery, and other military equipment to fight effectively. Demand for its chief export, cotton, declined and put its economy in jeopardy. The Confederate currency collapsed, and overseas credit was virtually impossible to get.

By the spring of 1865, the Confederacy was in disarray and close to collapse. In his second inaugural address in March, Lincoln spoke to this state of affairs and to the tough job of healing the nation that lay ahead. He stated:

> With malice toward none, with charity for all, with firm-
> ness in the right as God gives us to see the right, let us strive

Fighting among the Southern states and lack of resources had destroyed the Confederate campaign to successfully defend their secession from the United States. At the courthouse in Appomattox, Virginia, Confederate general Robert E. Lee *(right)* **officially surrendered to Union general Ulysses S. Grant** *(left)***. Other factions in the South would later put down their arms as well.**

on to finish the work we are in, to bind up the nation's wounds . . . to do all which may achieve and cherish a just and lasting peace among ourselves and with all nations.[6]

The next month, on April 4, Union troops entered the Confederate capital of Richmond. The president went there to view the situation himself. As Lincoln walked around the city, he was startled to see black laborers drop to their knees and praise him. Lincoln told them they must not kneel to him. He said that they should kneel to God only and that they should thank the Lord for the liberty they were about to enjoy.

A few days later, on April 9, 1865, Confederate general Robert E. Lee surrendered to Union general Ulysses S. Grant at Appomattox, Virginia. When the few remaining parts of the rebel armies surrendered later that month, the war finally was over.

The Thirteenth
Amendment

The Emancipation Proclamation was specifically, and only, a wartime measure. It was enforced for a particular emergency, at a clearly defined and unique period in the nation's history. It did not, therefore, guarantee the end of slavery.

When the war ended, it was not at all clear that slavery would be permanently banished. No legal restrictions prevented individual states or territories from reinstituting the practice. Nor was there a law to prevent a future federal administration from allowing slavery on a nationwide basis.

Because of this uncertainty, abolitionists were eager to pass a law to eliminate slavery throughout the nation and on a permanent basis. Lincoln was wholeheartedly behind this. Biographer Ida M. Tarbell wrote: "Mr. Lincoln believed that as soon as the war was over, the proclamation would become void. Voters would have to decide then what slaves it freed—whether only those who had under it made an effort for their freedom and had come into the Union lines or all of those in the States and parts of States in rebellion at the time it was issued."[1]

THE FIRST ATTEMPT

There was only one sure way for permanent abolition to happen. Congress and the individual states had to agree to make an amendment to the U.S. Constitution. Twelve amendments already existed, so a ban on slavery would be the Thirteenth Amendment.

In a strange historical twist, Congress had tried to pass a Thirteenth Amendment about slavery earlier—in 1861, while the war was still going on. This earlier proposed amendment actually had been designed to do just the opposite of the Thirteenth Amendment now being considered. It would have guaranteed that slavery would *never* be abolished. Known as the Corwin Amendment, it narrowly passed in both houses of Congress and was ratified by two states. However, the war had stopped the progress of this controversial legislation, and it never advanced far enough to become law.

The Senate Judiciary Committee was in charge of the matter. Senator Lyman Trumbull, who was a Republican from Illinois like Lincoln, chaired this committee. Trumbull and his colleagues were given the task of considering several abolition proposals that had come from a variety of sources. The committee then combined portions of three of these proposals to create a compromise amendment.

The amendment, as it finally appeared, is short and elegant in its simplicity. The entire text reads:

Section 1. Neither slavery nor involuntary servitude, except as a punishment for crime whereof the party shall have been duly convicted, shall exist within the United States, or any place subject to their jurisdiction.

Section 2. Congress shall have power to enforce this article by appropriate legislation.[2]

TRYING A SECOND TIME

In April 1864, a year before the end of the war and while Southern lawmakers were not present to vote, the U.S. Senate approved this compromise proposal. The vote was overwhelmingly in favor: 62 for it, 38 against it. The proposal, however, failed in the next step to becoming law. It could not get the necessary two-thirds majority of votes to pass in the House of Representatives.

The amendment proposal failed at this point, in part, because of the makeup of the House. Abolition primarily was a Republican concern, and most Democratic lawmakers seemed indifferent, if not actively opposed, to it. Only four Democratic congressmen voted for the proposed amendment.

Another reason it failed concerned the question of states' rights. Believers in states' rights held that individual states generally should have greater power and authority than the rights of a centralized federal government. States' rights advocates argued that each individual state should have the right to determine if it would or would not be a slave state.

In fact, a few states did individually deal with the question during this period. Notably, the border states of Maryland and Missouri elected to free their slaves before the war ended. Maryland's ban took effect in November 1864, and Missouri's was in place as of January 1865. In early 1865, a third slave state, Tennessee, also adopted an abolition amendment to its state constitution.

But the president was not willing to let individual states decide the matter. After the abolition amendment proposal was defeated in Congress in April 1864, Lincoln began putting pressure on his fellow politicians. He wanted to ensure that the proposal passed when it came up for vote again.

Right before the end of the Civil War, two candidates were nominated for the presidential election of 1864 to challenge Lincoln. General George B. McClellan and General John Frémont both ran for office under different parties, but were resoundingly defeated by Lincoln. *Above*, an election poster for the Democratic candidates, General George B. McClellan and his running mate, George Pendleton.

Lincoln made sure that the proposal was added to the Republican platform for the presidential elections of 1864. As expected, he was nominated for a second term. This was the contest that pitted him against the Democratic contender, the North's former top general, George B. McClellan, and another

THIRTEENTH AMENDMENT GETS LINCOLN REELECTED

Lincoln made the passage of the Thirteenth Amendment a cornerstone of his reelection campaign and of his second administration. On January 1, 1864, while the war was still going on, Lincoln's friend and Illinois congressman Isaac N. Arnold paid a New Year's Day call to him. According to Arnold's biography of Lincoln, he congratulated the president on recent military victories and the brightening prospects for peace. Arnold then said:

'I hope, Mr. President, that on next New Year's Day I have the pleasure of congratulating you on three events which now seem very probable.'

'What are they?' said he.

'First, that the war may be ended by the complete triumph of the Union forces. Second, that slavery may be abolished and prohibited throughout the Union by an amendment of the Constitution. Third, that Abraham Lincoln may have been re-elected President.'

'I think,' replied he, with a smile, 'I think, my friend, I would be willing to accept the first two by way of compromise.'*

---

* Isaac N. Arnold, The Life of Abraham Lincoln, Chicago, Ill.: A.C. McClurg, 1885, p. 351–352, reprinted on "13th Amendment," "Abraham Lincoln and Freedom," http://www.mrlincolnandfreedom.org/inside. asp?ID=56&subjectID=3.

former Union general, the Radical Republican John C. Frémont. Lincoln won the election in one of American history's greatest landslides. He captured all but 2 states, and garnered 212 out of 233 electoral votes.

"AN EXPLOSION, A STORM OF CHEERS"

Lincoln's massive win, combined with the failing fortunes of the Confederacy and the increasing dominance of the North in the war, helped the amendment proposal move ahead. After the elections, Lincoln made its passage a top priority for his second administration. The Senate already had approved it, and a majority in Congress now was in a mood to support it.

So, in a vote late in January 1865, the House of Representatives overwhelmingly approved the passage of the Thirteenth Amendment. The vote was 119 to 56, with 8 abstaining. Noah Brooks, a journalist and an early biographer of Lincoln, witnessed the scene in Congress when the votes were tallied. He recalled:

> For a moment there was a pause of utter silence. Then there was an explosion, a storm of cheers, the like of which probably no Congress of the United States ever heard before. Strong men embraced each other with tears. The galleries and aisles were bristling with standing, cheering crowds . . . women's handkerchiefs waving and floating; hands . . . shaking . . . arms about each other's necks, and cheer after cheer . . . burst after burst.[3]

THE DEATH OF LINCOLN

The next step for the proposed amendment began immediately. Early in 1865, Lincoln approved the amendment, and it was sent out to the individual state legislatures. The Constitution requires that three-quarters of the states ratify a proposed amendment before it can go into effect. (*Ratify* is a precise legal term meaning "approve." It comes from a Latin word for "fixed" or "valid.")

Meanwhile, in April the war ended. But then, as if the long and deadly conflict were not enough, still more tragedy struck. The president did not live to see the final approval of his amendment to end slavery forever. He could not witness the completion of the crowning achievement of his administration, one of the great moments in American history.

On April 14, 1865, just days after the formal end of the war, Abraham Lincoln was assassinated by John Wilkes Booth. Booth was a well-known actor, a Southerner, and a fervent advocate of the Confederacy.

Outraged at the South's defeat, Booth shot the president in the back of his head during a performance of the play *Our American Cousin* at Ford's Theatre. Lincoln died the next day, and his vice president, Andrew Johnson, succeeded him. (Johnson and Secretary of State Seward were targeted for assassination at the same time by Booth's colleagues, but these plans failed.)

Johnson pledged to carry on many of the policies that Lincoln had advocated. One of the most important of these was Reconstruction, an overall term for programs designed to repair the deep rift between the North and the South.

RATIFICATION

Reconstruction involved, in some cases, literally reconstructing parts of the South that had been left devastated and destitute by the war. Another important aspect involved creating institutions, such as schools, to help millions of newly freed slaves assimilate into mainstream America. And still another issue concerned federal legislation to protect the rights of black people, beginning with the Thirteenth Amendment.

All of these aspects of Reconstruction were daunting tasks, but especially the passage of legislation to alter the Constitution. The Constitution is perhaps the single most important and most revered document in American law and politics. Making a change to it is never taken lightly, and such a change,

After the Civil War, efforts were made to ease the transition between slavery and freedom. Government organizations and missionaries often contributed funds and resources for schools to help educate black children and adults in the South, establishing many Freedmen's Schools throughout the region.

in the form of an amendment, typically requires years of hard work and serious debate.

The adoption of a new amendment is therefore rare. In fact, as of 1865 there had been only 12 amendments, and all of them (including the first 10, known as the Bill of Rights) were adopted within 15 years after the Constitution was written. That meant that, when Congress approved the Thirteenth

Amendment, there had been no new constitutional amendments in more than 60 years.

Approval by the necessary majority of states was not a sure thing. At the time, there were 36 states in the Union—but 11 of those, more than a quarter of the total, were former slave states that recently had been in rebellion. They were unlikely to ratify the measure.

THE AMENDMENT BECOMES LAW

In order to make the amendment into law, therefore, it was necessary to convince some of the former rebel states to approve the amendment. This required long and hard work by pro-abolition statesmen. In the end, however, eight former Confederate states did approve it—even before they technically were states of the Union again.

By early March, the measure was approved by 19 states, mostly in the Midwest, New England, and the Mid-Atlantic region. The border states of Maryland, West Virginia, and Missouri, as well as two western states—Kansas and Nevada—also approved it. Three states—Delaware, Kentucky, and New Jersey—rejected it.

It took nearly a year before a majority of states ratified the Thirteenth Amendment. But it did get the majority it needed. Secretary of State Seward formally announced this on December 18, 1865, some eight months after Lincoln's assassination. With this, the last of America's slaves—about 1,000 in Delaware and an estimated 40,000 to 65,000 in Kentucky—finally became free.

MORE RECONSTRUCTION AMENDMENTS

More legislation, including two so-called Reconstruction Amendments, followed soon after. These laws were designed to protect the rights of former slaves.

Even after the Emancipation Proclamation gave slaves their freedom, life still was terribly difficult for them. They typically lived and worked in conditions nearly as poor as those they had lived in before the war, and they had precious few chances to better themselves. Not even such basic rights as citizenship and voting were guaranteed.

As might be expected, things were worse in the South than in the North. Lawmakers in Southern states were forced to allow emancipation, but they passed a variety of statutes that kept blacks as second-class citizens. (These discriminatory laws were collectively called Jim Crow laws, named for a popular song of the time.)

Such discriminatory laws were offset somewhat in 1866, when Congress passed the Civil Rights Act. This legislation granted citizenship to all native-born Americans (except Native Americans) and guaranteed "the same right in every state . . . to make and enforce contracts, to sue . . . to inherit, purchase, sell, and convey real and personal property; and to the full and equal benefit of all laws and proceedings for the security of person and property as is enjoyed by white citizens."[4]

The Civil Rights Act was followed two years later by stronger legislation. The Fourteenth Amendment, ratified in July 1868, was designed specifically to protect the civil rights of former slaves. In addition to including a broad definition of citizenship, the Fourteenth Amendment guaranteed such basic rights as due process and equal protection under the law.

THE RIGHT TO VOTE

The Fourteenth Amendment did not guarantee a full spectrum of rights. Notably, African Americans still were not guaranteed the right to vote. The Fifteenth Amendment closed this gap.

This amendment, which was ratified in February 1870, banned all racial restrictions on voting. In its entirety, it states:

> Section 1. The right of citizens of the United States to vote shall not be denied or abridged by the United States or by any State on account of race, color, or previous condition of servitude.

Section 2. The Congress shall have power to enforce this article by appropriate legislation.[5]

African Americans now had the vote—that is, African-American men did. Women (of any race) would not have the right to vote in the United States for another 50 years, until the Nineteenth Amendment was ratified in 1920.

Much was accomplished with the Emancipation Proclamation and the Reconstruction Amendments. At least in theory, African Americans were free citizens with equal civil rights. However, there still was much to do. This was because in practice—in "real life"—these newfound rights were not always honored. In the words of distinguished African-American attorney Charles Hamilton Houston, "Nobody needs to explain to a Negro the difference between the law in books and the law in action."[6]

The struggle to make all citizens genuinely equal has been ongoing, difficult, and often violent in the years since then. This struggle forms part of the legacy of the Emancipation Proclamation.

The Proclamation's Legacy

The Emancipation Proclamation, which Lincoln called "the central act of my administration, and the great event of the nineteenth century,"[1] had deep, widespread, and lasting effects. This was true in the short term, immediately after it was issued, and it continues to be true in the long term as well, over a century later.

In the short term, the proclamation accomplished its primary goal. It freed the slaves, turned the tide of the war in the North's favor, and so preserved the Union. In the long term, this dryly written, 713-word document changed forever the lives of millions of people and their descendants.

JUNETEENTH

On the other hand, the Emancipation Proclamation had little immediate effect on the daily lives of many slaves, especially

When Union soldiers finally reached Texas to declare freedom for all men, the day became known as Juneteenth. Every year, communities throughout the United States celebrate Juneteenth with parties, concerts, and picnics. *Above,* **trail boss James Frances Jr. leads the Emancipation Trail Ride, a Juneteenth event in Galveston, Texas.**

those in the Deep South. An example of this is the story behind Juneteenth.

On June 19, 1865, 2,000 Union soldiers arrived in Galveston, Texas, with news that the war was over and that the slaves were free. This news had traveled very slowly in the loyally Confederate state—the summer of 1865 was a full two and a half years after the Emancipation Proclamation had been issued.

When they heard the news, the slaves of Galveston erupted in spontaneous celebrations, and the news gradually spread to the state's 250,000 other slaves. In the following years, former slaves around Galveston continued to celebrate an annual holiday they called Juneteenth, in honor of that date. Families, friends, and church congregations gathered to rejoice, to have picnics and barbecues, and to pray and reflect on their freedom. The celebration spread to other parts of the country, although it remained centered around Galveston.

Interest in Juneteenth declined in the first part of the twentieth century. As it was across the country, the Fourth of July became the most commonly celebrated observance of independence. However, interest in Juneteenth returned in the 1970s, thanks to a renewed interest among black community members in the historical foundations of their freedom. In 1980, Juneteenth became an official holiday in Texas, and it has spread to other states in the years since. Today, Juneteenth celebrations happen in roughly half of the states in the United States, and it is an official state holiday in about half of those.

"THE PROBLEM OF THE TWENTIETH CENTURY"

Juneteenth is just one way in which the Emancipation Proclamation's impact on American life is still being felt and analyzed today. Lincoln was correct when he remarked, about signing the document, that "if my name ever goes into history, it will be for this act."[2]

Indeed, the Emancipation Proclamation today is considered one of the most important manuscripts in American history. Going even further, many observers consider it one of the great cornerstones of human freedom, of any place and any time. The Emancipation Proclamation is so important, history professor Allen C. Guelzo writes, that it can be thought of as "the single most far-reaching, even revolutionary, act of any American president."[3]

In the years immediately after the war, some of the peacetime effects of the proclamation, and of the legislation related to it, were clear. For example, in the period of Reconstruction following the end of the war, black people who had just been

THE REPUBLICAN PARTY AFTER THE WAR

After the war, the Republican Party mainly consisted of three groups—carpetbaggers (a term used by political opponents for politicians from the North who traveled to the South during Reconstruction), Southern whites who supported the Reconstruction process (called "scalawags" by the opposition), and freedmen (Southern blacks who were former slaves). Freedmen, firmly loyal to the party of Abraham Lincoln, made up the majority of the votes and served at nearly every level of government. Black officeholders were numerous, from the U.S. Congress, to the state legislatures, and to city councils and council commissions, with the largest number holding office in South Carolina.

Although they typically enacted laws that provided for civil and political rights regardless of race, these politicians were met with fierce opposition. Southern whites, still bitter over the loss of the war, opposed the high taxes they had to pay in support of Reconstruction programs. There also was a problem with political corruption that became associated with the Republican Party.

given the vote sent a number of African-American lawmakers to Congress for the first time.

But the Emancipation Proclamation clearly did not solve all of the many ongoing problems related to race. A great deal of work was necessary to help ex-slaves assimilate into mainstream American society and to adjust to their new lives. Similarly, a great deal of work was needed to help the white population adjust to the new order of things.

The questions of race relations and the struggle for equal civil rights for all were obviously going to be crucial and ongoing

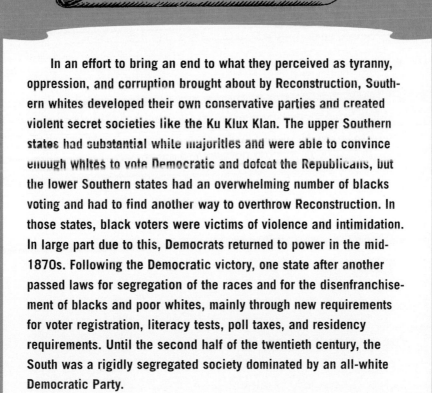

In an effort to bring an end to what they perceived as tyranny, oppression, and corruption brought about by Reconstruction, Southern whites developed their own conservative parties and created violent secret societies like the Ku Klux Klan. The upper Southern states had substantial white majorities and were able to convince enough whites to vote Democratic and defeat the Republicans, but the lower Southern states had an overwhelming number of blacks voting and had to find another way to overthrow Reconstruction. In those states, black voters were victims of violence and intimidation. In large part due to this, Democrats returned to power in the mid-1870s. Following the Democratic victory, one state after another passed laws for segregation of the races and for the disenfranchisement of blacks and poor whites, mainly through new requirements for voter registration, literacy tests, poll taxes, and residency requirements. Until the second half of the twentieth century, the South was a rigidly segregated society dominated by an all-white Democratic Party.

issues in the coming decades. As the distinguished black writer and intellectual W.E.B. Du Bois stated in 1903, "The problem of the twentieth century is the problem of the color line."[4]

GAINING LITTLE?

As the twentieth century continued, Du Bois's prediction came true. Life in America continued to be deeply unjust for African Americans as a whole. True equality was found almost nowhere. Some people, looking back with the knowledge of this inequality, became cynical about Lincoln's intentions.

In particular, a number of historians, intellectuals, and leaders began to rethink Lincoln's role in history. They argued that his intentions had never been to achieve equality for the races. They asked questions such as, Why did Lincoln take so long to sign the proclamation? And why did he limit its powers?

They argued that his declaration had been issued strictly for political and military expediency, not out of any true moral purpose. In an influential 1948 essay, leading historian Richard Hofstadter dismissed the Emancipation Proclamation as nothing more than a cynical political ploy and said that it had "the moral grandeur of a bill of lading [cargo]."[5] Hofstadter's attitude reflected that of many people concerning the realities of integration.

In the eyes of critics such as Hofstadter, the proclamation once had been inflammatory, brave, and controversial—but now was considered quite the opposite. Historian Harold Holzer comments, "A document that once struck many critics as radical, divisive, and dangerous, has more recently been assailed by skeptics as timid, conservative, and deceptive."[6]

THE CIVIL RIGHTS ERA BEGINS

It is true that, on a daily basis, much about the lives of black people in America remained grim. They still were subjected to serious forms of discrimination that touched nearly every aspect of their lives. In matters such as jobs, education, and housing, African Americans still were second-class citizens. Allen C. Guelzo points out, "By the time Hofstadter wrote off the Proclamation in 1948, American blacks had gained little from the Emancipation Proclamation beyond the bare fact of emancipation itself."[7]

For the first half of the twentieth century, blacks and whites still lived mostly segregated lives. This was true especially in the South, but it was true in parts of the North as well. By law or by custom, the races went to separate schools; lived in separate neighborhoods; sat in separate areas of theaters, stadiums, buses, and trains; used separate restrooms; and ate in separate restaurants. Furthermore, facilities such as hotels and restaurants for black people were almost invariably second rate.

Tensions between the races remained high, and sometimes it erupted into the open violence of riots, beatings, and even lynchings. The tension reached a fever pitch in the middle of the century, during the period known today as the Civil Rights Era. This was an era of organized protests that led to sweeping legislative acts and dramatic changes in black-white relationships. These legislative acts and societal changes were, of course, direct descendants of the Emancipation Proclamation. They could not have happened without it.

MONTGOMERY

There are disagreements over the exact years of the Civil Rights Era. Roughly speaking, however, this period of history lasted from the mid-1940s to the late 1960s. Some historians feel the era began when President Harry S. Truman fully desegregated the military in 1945 after the end of World War II. Others mark the beginning as dating from the Supreme Court decision of *Brown v. Board of Education* in 1954. This was a landmark ruling that struck down the long-held concept that "separate but equal" schools were acceptable.

Still others argue that the movement truly began with the Montgomery Bus Boycott of 1955 to 1956, the first large-scale

Rosa Parks, a black seamstress from Montgomery, Alabama, was arrested for her refusal to relinquish her bus seat to a white passenger. Her quiet action sparked the Montgomery bus boycott, a nonviolent protest against the public bus system led by Martin Luther King Jr. *Above*, **Rosa Parks is fingerprinted at a police station after her arrest.**

protest of the period. The Montgomery Bus Boycott was sparked when a woman named Rosa Parks refused to sit in the back of a public bus, as black people were required to do in Montgomery, Alabama, as well as in many other Southern cities. The dispute grew to involve months of protest in which virtually all of the city's black population refused to use the bus system. In the end, Montgomery was forced to desegregate its public transportation.

The Montgomery protest was notable in several ways. One of the most important was that it brought to national prominence a man who would soon become the symbol of the struggle for civil rights in America. This was the charismatic young Baptist minister named Dr. Martin Luther King Jr. who led the protest.

DR. KING AND CIVIL DISOBEDIENCE

In leading the bus boycott and the many other protests in which he was involved, King adopted the basic concepts of a philosophy called nonviolent civil disobedience. Civil disobedience involved making protests that deliberately disobeyed existing laws. Such tactics were not new—an activist in India, Mohandas Gandhi, had perfected them in the first half of the twentieth century. In 1945, Gandhi (often called Mahatma, a term of respect) led his country to independence from Great Britain through using mass civil disobedience to force political and social changes.

In addition to Gandhi's ideas about civil disobedience, King's philosophy also was based, in large part, on his deeply held beliefs in Christian love and compassion. These beliefs prohibited King from answering violence with violence. Although the struggle for civil rights attracted supporters from many religions and many walks of life, the movement's deepest roots were in the Christian concept of "turning the other cheek" to one's attackers. (It was no coincidence that so many of the era's civil rights leaders were, like King, also religious leaders.)

In time, King and his colleagues organized protests all over the country, lobbying for equality and justice for African Americans. Taken together, they formed the largest nonviolent protest movement in world history.

BUSES AND LUNCH COUNTERS

These protests took a number of forms. For example, a group of activists called the Freedom Riders rode in buses traveling between states, black and white sitting together despite integration restrictions in some states. Others sat at the lunch counters of Southern department stores reserved for whites, remaining there quietly until they were served.

As the movement gained momentum, these and other nonviolent protests were often met with violent opposition. Southern whites typically were outraged at the protests, and police often looked the other way when citizens took matters into their own hands. Beatings, bombings, mass jailings, intimidation, house burnings, and even murder became almost commonplace. But the activists persevered, and by doing so they forced a number of sweeping changes.

One of the most important changes was the Civil Rights Act of 1960, which strengthened voting rights for all citizens. It did so by requiring inspections of voter registration polls and setting penalties for anyone who tried to interfere with a person's right to vote. Also crucial was another amendment to the Constitution, the Twenty-fourth Amendment. Ratified in 1964, the Twenty-fourth Amendment outlawed poll taxes for national elections. Such taxes had been used in Southern states to keep black populations disenfranchised. The National Voting Rights Act of 1965 further strengthened ways in which the government could assure the rights of all citizens to vote. It outlawed the literacy tests that some states used to keep black populations from voting.

"I HAVE A DREAM"

For many, the civil rights movement was symbolized by a single event: a massive rally, called the March on Washington for Jobs and Freedom, which was held in the nation's capital in August 1963. Its central gathering place was—of course—the Lincoln Memorial. This monument in the National Mall had been dedicated in 1922 to the man who is often called the nation's greatest president.

Estimates put the crowd at the Lincoln Memorial on that day at between 200,000 and 300,000 people. They had come from all over the country. It was at this event that King made his famous "I Have a Dream" speech.

Like Abraham Lincoln, Martin Luther King Jr.'s eloquence and oratory skills inspired citizens to work together to overcome racial injustices. Lauded for his leadership skills, he was recognized as the leader of the civil rights movement and was awarded the Nobel Peace Prize for his use of nonviolent protest.

At the beginning of this speech, King paid explicit tribute to the Emancipation Proclamation, which had taken effect 100 years earlier. He acknowledged that the current struggle for civil rights never could have happened if the Emancipation Proclamation had not come first. Using the rousing oratory of his Baptist-ministerial background, King said:

> Five score years ago, a great American, in whose symbolic shadow we stand today, signed the Emancipation Proclamation. This momentous decree came as a great beacon light of hope to millions of Negro slaves who had been seared in the flames of withering injustice. It came as a joyous daybreak to end the long night of their captivity.[8]

"TOO GREAT A BURDEN"

That same year, there were many other observances in celebration of the Emancipation Proclamation's centennial year. Some of these were memorial speeches by the nation's leaders.

For example, President John F. Kennedy stated, "Surely, in 1963, 100 years after emancipation, it should not be necessary for any American citizen to demonstrate in the streets for an opportunity to stop at a hotel, or eat at a lunch counter . . . on the same terms as any other customer."[9] And, at the site of Lincoln's Gettysburg Address, Vice President Lyndon B. Johnson said, "Until justice is blind, until education is unaware of race, until opportunity is unconcerned with the color of men's skins, emancipation will be a proclamation but not a fact."[10]

As the decade wore on, frustrations about racial inequalities exploded more frequently into riots and other violence. By the late 1960s, nonviolent civil disobedience was starting to wane as the movement's dominant form of protest. Increasingly, members of the black community rejected King's philosophy of nonviolence and adopted one of militant confrontation. The slogan "Black Power" was coined and groups that condoned confrontation, such as the Black Panther Party and the Black Muslims, were on the rise.

King himself became a victim of the era's escalating violence when he was assassinated in Memphis, Tennessee, in 1968. To many within the civil rights movement, King's death was a devastating blow. It signaled the end of the civil rights movement—or at least the beginning of its end.

"ONE CAN ONLY HOPE"

Despite the shocking upset of King's murder, however, the fight for equality continued—and it continues to this day. In the decades since, African Americans have done amazing things, and have made amazing strides personally, politically, and socially. They have achieved goals that would have been unthinkable 50 or 100 years earlier. On November 4, 2008, Senator Barack Obama, the son of a black economist from Africa and a white anthropologist from Kansas, was elected the first African-American president of the United States.

And yet subtle forms of discrimination still do exist. Until this discrimination ends, Americans will need to draw inspiration from the proclamation that Abraham Lincoln made back in 1863. As the historian John Hope Franklin once remarked, "One can only hope that sooner rather than later we can all find the courage to live under the spirit of the Emancipation Proclamation and under the laws that flowed from its inspiration."[11]

CHRONOLOGY

1860   **November 6** Lincoln is elected president for the first time.

1861   **March 4** Lincoln is inaugurated.

       April 12–13 The attack on Fort Sumter, S.C., initiates the Civil War.

1862   **June–July** Lincoln writes the initial draft of the Emancipation Proclamation.

       July 22 Lincoln reads and discusses the draft at a meeting of his cabinet.

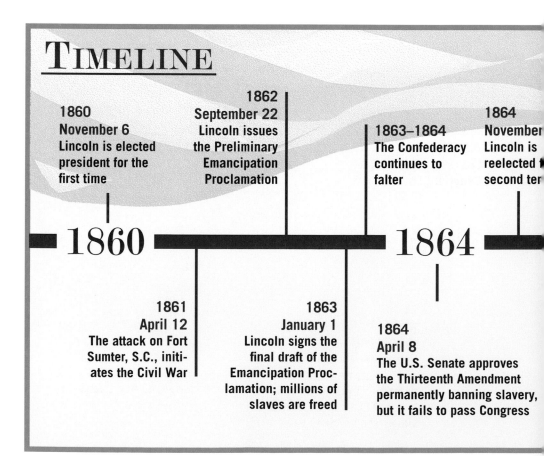

TIMELINE

1860
November 6
Lincoln is elected president for the first time

1862
September 22
Lincoln issues the Preliminary Emancipation Proclamation

1863–1864
The Confederacy continues to falter

1864
November
Lincoln is reelected
second ter

1860   **1864**

1861
April 12
The attack on Fort Sumter, S.C., initiates the Civil War

1863
January 1
Lincoln signs the final draft of the Emancipation Proclamation; millions of slaves are freed

1864
April 8
The U.S. Senate approves the Thirteenth Amendment permanently banning slavery, but it fails to pass Congress

September 17   The Battle of Antietam is fought. This gives Lincoln the opportunity to issue the Preliminary Emancipation Proclamation.

September 22   Lincoln prints and distributes the Preliminary Emancipation Proclamation.

1863   **January 1** Lincoln signs the final draft of the Emancipation Proclamation; millions of slaves are freed; hundreds of thousands of slaves join the Union Army; the course of the war changes to favor the Union.

November 19 Lincoln delivers the Gettysburg Address.

1865
January 31
Both House and Senate overwhelmingly approve the Thirteenth Amendment
April 9
Lee surrenders to Grant at Gettysburg; the war ends

1868
July 13
The Fourteenth Amendment is ratified, protecting the civil rights of former slaves

1865

1870

1865
April 14
Lincoln is assassinated
December 8
The Thirteenth Amendment is ratified and becomes law; the last of the nation's slaves are freed

1870
February 3
The Fifteenth Amendment is ratified, guaranteeing the right of all citizens to vote

NOTES

CHAPTER 1

1. Frank Donovan, *Mr. Lincoln's Proclamation: The Story of the Emancipation Proclamation*, New York, N.Y.: Dodd, Mead, 1964, 142.
2. Donovan, 76.
3. Philip B. Kunhardt, Jr., Philip B. Kunhardt III, and Peter W. Kunhardt, *Lincoln: An Illustrated Biography*, New York, N.Y.: Knopf, 1992, 114.
4. Mario Cuomo and Newt Gingrich, "Come to Cooper Union," *New York Sun*, February 27, 2007, http://www2.nysun.com/article/49402.
5. "Abraham Lincoln's Cooper Union Address," on Abraham Lincoln Online, http://showcase.netins.net/web/creative/lincoln/speeches/cooper.htm.
6. "Summary of Lincoln's Arguments at Cooper Union," Lincoln Home National Historic Site, http://www.nps.gov/liho/historyculture/summary.htm.
7. Abraham Lincoln Online.
8. Paul M. Angle, "Lincoln's Power with Words," http://www.historycooperative.org/journals/jala/3/angle.html.

CHAPTER 2

1. "Southern Free-Soilism," New York *Times*, July 23, 1856, http://query.nytimes.com/gst/abstract.html?res=9B01E3DB1339E134BC4B51DFB166838D649FDE.

2. Dr. Clayborne Carson, ed., *Civil Rights Chronicle: The African-American Struggle for Freedom*, Lincolnwood, Ill.: Publications Limited, 2003, 15.
3. Thomas Keneally, *Abraham Lincoln*, New York, N.Y.: Penguin, 2003, 65.
4. "John Brown," on "Africans in America," reprinted on http://www.pbs.org/wgbh/aia/part4/4p1550.html.
5. "The Avalon Project at Yale Law School," http://www.yale.edu/lawweb/avalon/csa/scarsec.htm.
6. William K. Klingaman, *Abraham Lincoln and the Road to Emancipation, 1861–1865.* New York, N.Y.: Penguin, 2001, 56.
7. Ibid., 60.
8. Ibid., 30.
9. "The Beginning of the End," *Harper's Weekly*, September 14, 1861, 578, http://mac110.assumption.edu/aas/Manuscripts/harpfremont.html.
10. Klingaman, p.76.
11. Edna Greene Medford, in Harold Holzer, Edna Greene Medford, and Frank J. Williams, *The Emancipation Proclamation: Three Views*. Baton Rouge, La.: Louisiana State University Press, 2006.
12. Klingaman, 148.
13. Ibid., 108.
14. Ida M. Tarbell, *The Life of Abraham Lincoln*, 110, http://books.google.com/books?id=b-

pDO5vQUYEC&pg=RA1-
PA110&lpg=RA1-PA110&dq=
"I+was+nearly+inconsolable+
as+I+could+be+and+live."
&source=web&ots=cFS7YdZRqu
&sig=gHm6rSqpNZUdUEoWit
c8t_pKAck&hl=en.

15. Klingaman, 153.

16. Allen C. Guelzo, *Lincoln's
Emancipation Proclamation: The
End of Slavery in America*, New
York, N.Y.: Simon & Schuster,
2004, 5.

17. Kunhardt, 166.

18. Carl Sandburg, *Abraham
Lincoln: The Prairie Years and
the War Years*, New York, N.Y.:
Harcourt Brace, 1954, 318.

19. Klingaman, 81.

20. Donovan, 74.

21. Klingaman, 1.

CHAPTER 3

1. Richard Striner, *Father Abraham:
Lincoln's Relentless Struggle to
End Slavery*, New York, N.Y.:
Oxford University Press, 2006, 7.

2. Henry Ketcham, *The Life of
Abraham Lincoln*, Whitefish,
Mont.: Kessinger Publishing,
2003, 142.

3. Ibid., 140.

4. "The Second Confiscation
Act," July 17, 1862. http://www.
history.umd.edu/Freedmen/
conact2.htm.

5. Klingaman, 140.

6. Ibid., 2.

7. Doris Kearns Goodwin, *Team
of Rivals: The Political Genius of
Abraham Lincoln*, New York, N.Y.:
Simon & Schuster, 2005, 459.

8. David Herbert Donald, *Lincoln*,
New York, N.Y.: Simon &
Schuster, 1995, 364.

9. Kunhardt, 196.

10. Goodwin, 464.

11. Klingaman, 187.

12. Guelzo, 8.

13. Klingaman, 181.

14. Ibid., 191.

15. Ibid.

16. Goodwin, 467.

CHAPTER 4

1. Francis Fisher Browne, *The
Every-Day Life of Abraham
Lincoln*, New York, N.Y.:
N.D. Thompson, 1887, 546,
http://books.google.com/
books?id=Bi8DAAAAYAAJ&
pg=PA546&lpg=PA546&dq=
"Seward+insisted+that+we+
ought+to+take+this+ground%
3B+and+the+words+finally+
went+in!%22&source=web&
ots=VNBFuGzx3N&sig=
pXMDD-3vuUjHAW4AfePSW
ZHIGf0&hl=en.

2. Goodwin, 468.

3. Ibid., 481.

4. Donovan, 109.

5. *Emancipation Proclamation—1862.* http://
www.civilwar-history.com/
Emancipation-Proclamation.
aspx.

6. Kunhardt, 197.

7. Donovan, 118–119.

8. John Hope Franklin, "The
Emancipation Proclamation:
An Act of Justice," reprinted on
"Prologue: Selected Articles,"
Prologue magazine, http://www.
archives.gov/publications/
prologue/1993/summer/

emancipation-proclamation. html.

9. Klingaman, 228.

10. "Gen. Curtis' Department," *New York Times*, December 28, 1862, 6, reprinted on http://query. nytimes.com/gst/abstract. html?res=9E0DEFD91331E03A BC4051DFB4678389679FDE.

11. Klingaman, 289.

12. Ibid.

13. Joseph E. Stevens, *1863 The Rebirth of a Nation*, New York, N.Y.: Bantam, 1999. Reprinted at http://extras.denverpost. com/books/ch18630801.htm.

14. "Civil War and the Capital City," *Washington Post*, February 24, 2004, reprinted at http://209. 85.173.104/search?q=cache: b1pkDL-vqeQJ:www.washpost. com/nielessonplans.nsf/0/ 4649318C51C078BA85256 E44006CFF02/%24File/ 5-CivilWarFinal.pdf+%22 departure+from+the+ thralldom+%22&hl=en&ct= clnk&cd=2&gl=us.

CHAPTER 5

1. "Emancipation Proclamation 1863," http://www.archives. gov/exhibits/american_ originals_iv/sections/ emancipation_proclamation. html.

2. Striner, 186.

3. "Emancipation Proclamation Background Information," on http://www.civilwarhome. com/emancipationbackground. htm.

4. Ibid.

5. Ibid.

6. Klingaman, 235.

7. Ibid., 196.

8. Striner, 201.

9. Klingaman, 197–98.

10. "Lincoln and Emancipation," http://www.civilwarhome. com/lincolnandproclamation. htm.

11. "Emancipation Proclamation Background Information."

12. Ibid.

13. Donovan, 113.

14. "Emancipation Proclamation Background Information."

15. "Lincoln and Emancipation."

16. Victoria Stubbs, "Emancipation Day: Let freedom ring," *The Thomaston (GA) Times*, May 23, 2008, reprinted on http://www.thomastontimes. com/articles/2008/05/23/news/ local1.txt.

CHAPTER 6

1. Guelzo, 1.

2. Klingaman, 111.

3. Howard Zinn, *A People's History of the United States: 1492– Present*. New York, N.Y.: HarperCollins, 1980, 192.

4. "Emancipation Proclamation Background Information."

5. Ibid.

6. Klingaman, 288.

CHAPTER 7

1. Ibid., 243.

2. Donald, 431.

3. John Rhodehamel, "Forever Free: Curator's Note," reprinted on http://ublib.buffalo.edu/ libraries/exhibits/ForeverFree/ curator.htm.

4. James M. McPherson, *The Atlas of the Civil War*, Philadelphia, Penn.: Running Press, 2005, 143.
5. "Second Inaugural Address of Abraham Lincoln," in *The Avalon Project at Yale Law School*, http://www.yale.edu/lawweb/avalon/presiden/inaug/lincoln2.htm.
6. Ida M. Tarbell, *The Life of Abraham Lincoln, Volume II*, New York, N.Y.: McClure, Phillips, 1900, 214, reprinted on http://www.mrlincolnandfreedom.org/inside.asp?ID=56&subjectID=3.

CHAPTER 8

1. "13th Amendment to the U.S. Constitution," http://www.nps.gov/archive/malu/documents/amend13.htm.
2. Isaac N. Arnold, *The Life of Abraham Lincoln*, Chicago, Ill.: A.C. McClurg, 1885, 351–352, reprinted on "13th Amendment," "Abraham Lincoln and Freedom," http://www.mrlincolnandfreedom.org/inside.asp?ID=56&subjectID=3.

3. Allen C. Guelzo, "'The Great Event of the Nineteenth Century': Lincoln Issues the Emancipation Proclamation." The Historical Society of Pennsylvania, http://www.hsp.org/default.aspx?id=570.
4. "Transcript of the Third Democratic Primary Presidential Debate," *The New York Times*, June 28, 2007, reprinted on http://www.nytimes.com/2007/06/28/us/politics/29transcript.html?_r=1&oref=slogin.
5. Guelzo, 2.
6. Holzer, "Introduction," in Holzer et al., xi.
7. Guelzo, "The Emancipation Proclamation: Bill of Lading or Ticket to Freedom?" History Now. http://www.historynow.org/12_2005/historian.html.
8. "The I Have a Dream Speech," U.S. Constitution Online, http://www.usconstitution.net/dream.html.
9. "The Emancipation Proclamation: An Act of Justice."
10. Ibid.
11. Ibid.

BIBLIOGRAPHY

BOOKS

Basler, Roy P., ed. *The Collected Works of Abraham Lincoln, Volume V.* Cleveland, Ohio: World Publishing, 1946.

Bennett Jr., Lerone. *Forced into Glory: Abraham Lincoln's White Dream.* Chicago, Ill.: Johnson Publishing, 2000.

Browne, Francis Fisher. *The Every-Day Life of Abraham Lincoln.* New York: N.D. Thompson, 1887 (reprinted on Google Books Online).

Carnahan, Burrus M. *Act of Justice: Lincoln's Emancipation Proclamation and the Law of War.* Lexington, Ky.: University Press of Kentucky, 2007.

Carson, Dr. Clayborne, ed. *Civil Rights Chronicle: The African-American Struggle for Freedom.* Lincolnwood, Ill.: Legacy, 2003.

Cuomo, Mario M. and Harold Holzer, eds. *Lincoln on Democracy.* New York: HarperCollins, 1990.

Donald, David Herbert. *Lincoln.* New York: Simon & Schuster, 1995.

Donovan, Frank. *Mr. Lincoln's Proclamation: The Story of the Emancipation Proclamation.* New York: Dodd, Mead, 1964.

Goodwin, Doris Kearns. *Team of Rivals: The Political Genius of Abraham Lincoln.* New York: Simon & Schuster, 2005.

Guelzo, Allen C. *Lincoln's Emancipation Proclamation: The End of Slavery in America.* New York: Simon & Schuster, 2004.

Holzer, Harold, Edna Greene Medford, and Frank J. Williams. *The Emancipation Proclamation: Three Views.* Baton Rouge, La.: Louisiana State University Press, 2006.

Jaffa, Harry V. "The Emancipation Proclamation," in Don E. Fehrenbacher, ed., *The Leadership of Abraham Lincoln*. New York: John Wiley and Sons, 1970.

Johnson, Michael P., ed. *Abraham Lincoln, Slavery, and the Civil War*. Boston: Bedford/St. Martin's, 2001.

Keneally, Thomas. *Abraham Lincoln*. New York: Penguin, 2002.

Klingaman, William K. *Abraham Lincoln and the Road to Emancipation, 1861–1865*. New York: Penguin, 2001.

Kunhardt Jr., Philip B., Philip B. Kunhardt III, Peter W. Kunhardt. *Lincoln: An Illustrated Biography*. New York: Knopf, 1992.

McPherson, James M. *Atlas of the Civil War*. Philadelphia: Running Press, 2005.

Miller, William Lee. *Lincoln's Virtues: An Ethical Biography*. New York: Knopf, 2002.

Neely, Jr., Mark A. *The Fate of Liberty: Abraham Lincoln and Civil Liberties*. New York: Oxford University Press, 1991.

Sandburg, Carl. *Abraham Lincoln: The Prairie Years and the War Years*. New York: Harcourt Brace, 1954.

Smith, Page. *Trial by Fire: A People's History of the Civil War and Reconstruction*. New York: McGraw-Hill, 1982.

Stevens, Joseph E. *1863: The Rebirth of a Nation*. New York: Bantam, 1999.

Striner, Richard. *Father Abraham: Lincoln's Relentless Struggle to End Slavery*. New York: Oxford University Press, 2006.

Tarbell, Ida M. *The Life of Abraham Lincoln*. New York: McClure, Phillips, 1900.

Vorenberg, Michael. *Final Freedom: The Civil War, the Abolition of Slavery, and the Thirteenth Amendment*. New York: Cambridge University Press, 2001.

Williams, Juan. *Eyes on the Prize: America's Civil Rights Years, 1954–1965*. New York: Penguin, 1987.

Zinn, Howard. *A People's History of the United States: 1492– Present*. New York: HarperCollins, 2003.

PERIODICALS AND WEB SITES

"13th Amendment to the U.S. Constitution." Available online. URL: http://www.nps.gov/archive/malu/documents/ amend13.htm.

Angle, Paul M. "Lincoln's Power with Words," Available online. URL: http://www.historycooperative.org/journals/jala/3/ angle.html.

"The Avalon Project at Yale Law School." Available online. URL: http://www.yale.edu/lawweb/avalon/csa/scarsec.htm.

"The Beginning of the End." *Harper's Weekly*, September 14, 1861. Available online. URL: http://mac110.assumption.edu/ aas/Manuscripts/harpfremont.html.

"Civil War and the Capital City." *Washington Post*, February 24, 2004. Available online. URL: http://www.washpost.com/ nielessonplans.nsf/0/4649318C51C078BA85256E44006CFF02/ $File/ 5-CivilWarFinal.pdf.

Cuomo, Mario and Newt Gingrich. "Come to Cooper Union." *New York Sun*, February 27, 2007. Available online. URL: http://www.nysun.com/opinion/come-to-cooper-union/ 49402/.

"Emancipation Proclamation—1862." Available online. URL: http://www.civilwar-history.com/Emancipation- Proclamation.aspx.

"Emancipation Proclamation Background Information." Available online. URL: http://www.civilwarhome.com/ emancipationbackground.htm.

"U.S. Constitution: Fourteenth Amendment." *Find-Law.* Available online. URL: http://caselaw.lp.findlaw.com/data/constitution/amendment14/.

Franklin, John Hope. "The Emancipation Proclamation: An Act of Justice." "Prologue: Selected Articles," *Prologue* magazine. Available online. URL: http://www.archives.gov/publications/prologue/1993/summer/emancipation-proclamation.html.

"Gen. Curtis' Department." *New York Times,* December 28, 1862. Available online. URL: http://query.nytimes.com/gst/abstract.html?res=9E0DEFD91331E03ABC4051DFB467838 9679FDE.

Guelzo, Allen. "The Emancipation Proclamation: Bill of Lading or Ticket to Freedom?" *History Now.* Available online. URL: http://www.historynow.org/12_2005/historian.html.

———. ""The Great Event of the Nineteenth Century': Lincoln Issues the Emancipation Proclamation." *The Historical Society of Pennsylvania.* Available online. URL: http://www.hsp.org/default.aspx?id=570.

"John Brown." *Africans in America.* Available online. URL: http://www.pbs.org/wgbh/aia/part4/4p1550.html.

King Jr., Martin Luther. "The American Dream." *The MLK Papers Project.* Available online. URL: http://www.stanford.edu/group/King/publications/sermons/650704_The_American_Dream.html.

———. "The I Have a Dream Speech." *U.S. Constitution Online.* Available online. URL: http://www.usconstitution.net/dream.html.

Lincoln, Abraham. "Abraham Lincoln's Cooper Union Speech." *Abraham Lincoln Online.* Available online. URL:

http://showcase.netins.net/web/creative/lincoln/speeches/
cooper.htm.

"Lincoln and Emancipation." Available online. URL: http://
www.civilwarhome.com/lincolnandproclamation.htm.

Lincoln, Abraham. "Emancipation Proclamation 1863." Available online. URL: http://www.archives.gov/exhibits/american_
originals_iv/sections/emancipation_proclamation.html.

Rhodehamel, John. "Forever Free: Curator's Note." Available
online. URL: http://ublib.buffalo.edu/libraries/exhibits/
ForeverFree/curator.htm.

"Southern Free-Soilism." *New York Times*, July 23, 1856. Available online. URL: http://query.nytimes.com/gst/abstract.
html?res=9B01E3DB1339E134BC4B51DFB166838D649FDE.

Stubbs, Victoria. "Emancipation Day: Let freedom ring."
Thomaston (GA) Times, May 23, 2008.

"Summary of Lincoln's Arguments at Cooper Union." *Lincoln
Home National Historic Site*. Available online. URL: http://
www.nps.gov/liho/historyculture/summary.htm.

"The Thirteenth Amendment: The Abolition of Slavery."
Exploring Constitutional Conflicts. Available online. URL:
http://www.law.umkc.edu/faculty/projects/ftrials/conlaw/
thirteenthamendment.html.

"Transcript of the Third Democratic Primary Presidential
Debate." *New York Times*, June 28, 2007. Available online.
URL: http://www.nytimes.com/2007/06/28/us/politics/
29transcript.html?_r=1&oref=slogin.

FURTHER READING

Graves, Karen Marie. *The Importance of Abraham Lincoln.* San Diego: Lucent, 2003.

Phillips, E.B. *Abraham Lincoln: From Pioneer to President.* New York: Sterling, 2007.

Sullivan, George. *Abraham Lincoln.* New York: Scholastic, 2000.

WEB SITES

Abraham Lincoln Online.

http://showcase.netins.net/web/creative/lincoln.html

Provides details of the many activities still going on related to Lincoln, his life, and his achievements.

HarpWeek: "13th Amendment Site."

http://www.harpweek.com/07Features/features.asp

Maintained by the magazine *Harper's Weekly,* which covered the issue in detail in the 1860s and is still publishing, this site has detailed information and analysis from the magazine's pages.

National Archives & Records Administration: "The Emancipation Proclamation."

http://www.archives.gov/exhibits/featured_documents/emancipation_proclamation/

This site is maintained by the National Archives and includes photos of Lincoln's handwritten proclamation.

Photo Credits

INDEX

Adams, Henry, 61–62
American Anti-Slavery
    Society, 49
Antietam, Battle of, 36–37
Appomattox, Virginia, 75
Arnold, Isaac N., 80–81
assassination of Abraham
    Lincoln, 81–82
Auld, Hugh, 48

Bates, Edward, 34, 42
Beecher, Henry Ward, 5
Bill of Rights, 83
Black Muslims, 99
Black Panther Party, 99
Black Power, 98
Blair, Montgomery, 34
Board of Education, Brown v., 93
Booth, John Wilkes, 82
border states
    abolition in, 78
    concerns over, 18–19, 21, 24
    Preliminary Emancipation
        Proclamation and, 40
boycotts, 93–95
Breckinridge, John, 10
Brooks, Noah, 81
Brown, John, 15, 59
Brown v. Board of Education, 93
Bureau of Colored Troops, 72
bus boycott, 93–95
Butler, Benjamin, 16–18

carpetbaggers, 90
Chase, Salmon P., 10, 34, 41
citizenship, slaves and, 13
civil disobedience, 95–96
Civil Rights Acts, 85, 96

Civil Rights Era, 92–99
Civil War, end of, 73–75
Columbian Orator, The, 48
compensation, emancipation
    and, 30, 45
Confederacy, effect of loss of
    slaves on, 66–68
Confiscation Acts, 18–19, 23
confiscation of slaves, 16–19,
    23, 33–34
constitutionalism, 4–6
content of Final Emancipation
    Proclamation, 44–45
Cooper Union speech,
    6–7, 30
Copperhead Democrats, 21
Corwin Amendment, 77–78
cotton, Great Britain and, 60
Covey, Edward, 48

Davis, Jefferson
    black Union soldiers
        and, 69
    Fort Sumter and, 15
    proclamation of for freeing
        slaves, 61
    reaction of to Emancipation
        Proclamation, 54, 58
debates, Lincoln-Douglas, 2
Douglas, Stephen, 2, 10
Douglass, Frederick, 15, 47,
    48–49
Draft Riot, 56–57
DuBois, W.E.B., 92

Eaton, John, 65–66
Eckert, Thomas T., 25
education, 12, 48

emancipation, gradual, 4, 7, 27
Emerson, Ralph Waldo, 47
enforcement, 39, 51
Europe, reactions in to Emancipation Proclamation, 59–62
Exeter Hall, London, 61

Ford's Theater, 82
Fort Pillow Massacre, 69–70
Forten, Charlotte, 50–51
Founding Fathers, 6–7
Fourteenth Amendment, 85–86
France, 59, 73
Franklin, John Hope, 99
free Negroes, 13–14
freedmen, 90
freedom, Preliminary Emancipation Proclamation and, 33, 35, 40
Freedom Riders, 95
Frémont, John C., 18, 62, 71, 81

Gandhi, Mohandas "Mahatma," 95
Garibaldi, Giuseppe, 59
Garrison, William Lloyd, 56
Gettysburg, Battle of, 67
gradual emancipation, 4, 7, 27
Grant, Ulysses S., 75
Great Britain, 59–61
Greeley, Horace, 8, 21, 22–23, 53

Halleck, Henry, 18, 53
Hamlin, Hannibal, 10, 28
Herndon, William, 6
Higginson, Thomas Wentworth, 21, 70–72

Hofstadter, Richard, 92
Holzer, Harold, 92
Houston, Charles Hamilton, 85
Hume, David, 12
Hunter, David, 70–71

Jefferson, Thomas, 5, 7
Jim Crow Laws, 85
jobs, competition for, 56
Johnson, Andrew, 72, 82
Johnson, Hannah, 47–48
Johnson, Lyndon B., 98
Jones, Charles Colcock, Jr., 58
Juneteenth, 87–89

Kennedy, John F., 98
King, Martin Luther, Jr., 95–99
Ku Klux Klan, 91

Lee, Robert E., 36, 75
Lincoln, Abraham
    Cooper Union speech of, 6–7
    death of, 81–82
    debates and, 2
    election of, 10
    opposition of to slavery, 1–5, 22–23
    Preliminary Emancipation Proclamation and, 25–38
    reelection of, 80–81
Lincoln Memorial, 96–98
Lincoln-Douglas debates, 2
literacy tests, 91
Longfellow, Henry Wadsworth, 47

March on Washington for Jobs and Freedom, 96–98
Marx, Karl, 59
McClellan, George B., 36, 62, 80

Monroe, Fort, 16
Montgomery Bus Boycott,
  93–95

Napoleon, Louis, 59
National Voting Rights Act, 96
Negro Soldier Law, 68
New York City Draft Riot, 56–57
newspapers, 8
North, slavery in, 13–14

Parks, Rosa, 94
Pillow (Fort) Massacre, 69–70
poll taxes, 91, 96
Preliminary Emancipation
  Proclamation
    annual message to Congress
      and, 40–41
    content of, 30–34
    issuing of, 37–38
    reactions to, 34–35
    Seward and, 35–36
    shortcomings of, 39–40
    writing of, 25–30
private property, slaves as, 12,
  16–19

Reconstruction Amendments,
  84–85
Republican Party after Civil War,
  90–91
residency requirements, 91
responses to Final Emancipation
  Proclamation, 46–51, 53–62,
  64–66
revolts, slaves and, 12
Rosecrans, William, 46

Saxton, Camp, 50–51
scalawags, 90
Schurz, Carl, 59
Scott, Dred, 14

secession, election of Lincoln
  and, 10, 15
Second Confiscation Act, 18–19,
  23, 33–34
segregation, 85, 91, 93
Seward, Fred, 42
Seward, William Henry
  as assassination target, 82
  election of Lincoln and, 10
  Final Emancipation
    Proclamation and, 41–42
  on length of Civil War, 16
  Preliminary Emancipation
    Proclamation and, 28, 34,
    35–36
Sharpsburg, Battle of. See
  Antietam, Battle of
slaves, reaction of to
  Emancipation Proclamation,
  64–66
Smith, Caleb B., 34
soldiers, blacks as, 68–73
Soldiers' Home, 28, 37
South, slavery in, 12
South Carolina, 15–16,
  50–51, 90
Stanton, Edwin M., 34
states, slavery and, 7, 78
Stowe, Harriet Beecher, 15, 47
Sumter, Fort, 15–16

Thirteenth Amendment
  first attempt at, 77–78
  as law, 84
  need for, 76–77
  passage of, 81
  ratification of, 82–84
  second attempt at, 78–81
Truman, Harry S., 93
Trumbull, Lyman, 77–78
Tubman, Harriet, 14
Turner, Henry M., 46–47

Turner, Nat, 14
Twenty-fourth Amendment, 96

Uncle Tom's Cabin (Stowe), 15
Underground Railroad, 14
Union Army, 53–54, 56–57

Vicksburg, Battle of, 67
voting rights, 13, 85–86, 91, 96

Wadsworth, William H., 19
warships, 60–61
wartime measure, emancipation
    as, 26, 42, 76
Washington, George, 6, 12
Welles, Gideon, 28, 55
Whiting, William, 26

Yates, Richard, 19

ABOUT THE AUTHOR

ADAM WOOG has written more than 60 books for adults, young adults, and children. He is especially interested in history and biography. Woog lives in Seattle, Washington, with his wife, a mental health therapist, and their daughter.